Martial Arts Masters

Martial Arts Masters

*Black Belt
Warriors
for Peace*

by Terrence Webster-Doyle

Weatherhill

First edition, 2001

Published by Weatherhill, Inc., 41 Monroe Turnpike, CT 06611. Protected by copyright under the terms of the International Copyright Union; all rights reserved. Except for fair use in book reviews, no part of this book may be reproduced for any reason by any means, including any method of photographic reproduction, without permission of Weatherhill, Inc. Printed in China.

05 04 03 02 01 8 7 6 5 4 3 2 1

Book and cover design by Mariana Canelo.

ISBN 0-8348-0487-5

Library of Congress CIP data available

Contents

Preface

Dear Reader,

This book is about martial arts that are for peace. It will teach you to resolve conflict peacefully, which is the true intent of all martial arts. It will also introduce you to the Martial Arts Code of Conduct, which all martial artists for peace have to understand in order to master these arts.

What is written here may at first seem difficult to understand. That's because it's probably new to you and like anything new it takes time and effort to absorb. If you are serious and want to study the martial arts to be a Black Belt Warrior for Peace then you will have to practice. Learning the martial arts takes time.

But if you keep at it, one day you will completely understand what is being said here. As you come to understand, your life will change for the better. This is because the martial arts that are for peace are meant to help you in your everyday life—to resolve conflict, to build character, and to create peace.

Respectfully,

Terrence Webster-Doyle ("Doctor T")

The young man was approached by an old warrior.

"What will you do to escape my power?" asked the old warrior.

"Nothing," replied the young man.

The Story of Henry

Defeating the Bully, The Smart Way

I want to tell you a story about Henry. Henry was a bright young man who went to an ordinary school in an ordinary town. And what happened to him at school was also ordinary, for we know that what happened to Henry happens to many young people in schools all over the world. But the out-of-the-ordinary thing Henry did was to get help.

It was just another day at school when Henry saw them again, the three jocks that bullied him constantly. Henry felt that knot in the pit of his stomach and the rage that started to boil up from deep inside. But he couldn't do anything. Henry wasn't fast so he couldn't run away from them. He wasn't big enough to stand up to them, especially since there were three of them. All he could do was to take it, like he always did. They would take his money, punch him, and sometimes even stuff him into his locker, which really hurt. But what hurt even more than being so badly bullied was that no one seemed to care. Everyone just pretended that nothing was going on.

Henry's stomach knotted tighter as he saw them coming closer. But this particular day Henry shut his eyes for a moment and imagined what he would really do to those bullies if he were tough enough. In his mind's eye Henry could see himself standing there looking confident and strong, like a movie hero. Henry watched Rambo and other action movies constantly, and had been dreaming about his revenge for a long time. He couldn't wait until they tried something.

Henry imagined the bullies about to grab him when all that pent-up rage came out in a flashing sidekick to Randy, the biggest jock. The powerful blow would send Randy staggering backward. Henry would then step up quickly and hit Randy with a reverse punch to the midsection. Randy would fall on the ground groaning and asking for mercy. Then as swiftly as Henry defended himself against Randy he would turn and with the swiftness of a tiger strike Tyler with a spinning hook kick. Tyler was another jock lineman who never showed mercy to anyone when playing football. He would spin around from the kick's impact and Henry would go after him with no mercy, just like the bullies did when they picked on him. The third bully was Jake, who by now would be standing there looking shocked and scared. Henry would advance quickly toward Jake, who would retreat rapidly. Henry envisioned himself standing there in a powerful combat stance looking at his conquered foes. "I'm in control; they're defeated," he thought. "They'll never bother me again!" Henry would feel proud, a champion, the cool action hero who dealt swiftly with his enemies, the kind of person he had always dreamed of being . . .

But Henry had been watching too many action movies, and had a vivid imagination. A strong hand on Henry's shoulder suddenly yanked him out of his daydream.

"OK, punk. Where's the money? You owe me big time, with interest. Let's have it," the threatening voice commanded.

Randy was staring Henry down. Randy was big and mean, and had told him before that he hated wimps like Henry, a nerd who didn't play sports but would rather read books. Henry closed his eyes again, but this time he was waiting for the beating he knew he would get and couldn't do anything about.

"Hey, guys. What's happening?" A cheery voice came from behind the three bullies. Henry opened his eyes to see an older kid whose name was Lamar Jackson. Lamar was only thirteen, but big and tall for his age. Henry didn't know him well since Lamar was two grades ahead of him, but he had heard that Lamar studied martial arts.

"What's it to you?" Randy and his pals turned to look at who was talking to them.

"Just wanted to tell you what a great game that was." Lamar went on in a friendly but powerful voice.

To Henry the moment seemed frozen in time. There he was, being held down by the strong arms of Randy and his two pals, while all four stared intently at this guy who had just butted in as he was about to take a beating.

Lamar then walked right up to Randy and put his hand out. "I'm Lamar and I know who you are. I've watched you play ball. You're really good. Saw the game with Harrison. That tackle you made saved the game. Really cool." Lamar spoke in a calm and reassuring manner. "And you're Tyler, and you're Jake. You guys are awesome too! I really like football but I don't have time to go out for it since I'm taking martial arts classes most every day. Going up for my first-degree black belt this summer. Anyway, you guys sure are fantastic athletes," he continued on in the same casual and confident way.

Randy, Tyler, and Jake were obviously pleased with the compliments Lamar was handing out. Randy's grip on Henry relaxed, and for the moment the bullies forgot all about him.

"Man, what about the game with Saunders? Was that amazing? How did you guys win that one? They were one tough team. Coach must really be proud of you. And I'm sure he thinks you're great, you know, good sportsmen, like having good school spirit, being models for all the students who look up to you. Everyone looks up to you guys for being leaders. I know all the younger kids really admire you. You guys are their heroes. Come to think of it, that's a lot of responsibility, being looked up to," Lamar went on.

"Yeah, it's pretty neat to be looked up to by the other guys," Randy said looking all puffed up and proud. He noticed that some kids were stopping to watch what was happening so he let go of Henry.

"Well, it was cool meeting a fan," Randy said to Lamar, not even taking any notice of Henry anymore. "But we can't stand here yakking all day. We have to get to practice, so see you later," Tyler and Jake looked toward Henry for a moment but he could see in their eyes that now he wasn't even worth their attention.

Henry saw Lamar the next day at lunch. He wanted to thank him for what he had done. As Henry came up to him, Lamar turned to Henry in that same friendly, casual way as before and invited him to sit down.

"Mental martial arts," he said before Henry could even thank him. "It's the only way out of a situation like that. I couldn't help you get away, so I got them to back off by using my brain instead of my fists, by talking our way out of it."

"You mean that was the martial arts?" Henry answered with astonishment. "Say, are you really going up for black belt? Could you kick their butts? I sure want to. I want to be like those action film heroes—do some flying kicks and knock them into tomorrow. I've seen them do that in the movies. It's really cool."

"No, not cool. That's not real martial arts, and they're not real martial artists, just a bunch of actors pretending to be tough. That's Hollywood. Make believe. A real martial artist is for peace. A real martial artist's goal is to stop conflict, *not* to fight."

"But that's not what the movies are about. They show the good guys totally wiping out the bad guys. The bad guys deserve it, don't they? I mean, it's an eye for an eye," Henry replied.

"C'mon, lots of people do something bad at one time or another. That doesn't mean they deserve to be killed. And real heroes don't always have to kick butt—there are lots of ways to defeat someone without bloodshed. But that doesn't thrill people, it doesn't sell. The movies are setups. They make the villains super mean and evil just to get you all worked up, to make you feel angry and afraid. So when the hero comes along and wastes the bad guy you feel better. The bad guy deserves it, so you feel good that you got revenge. But real life isn't like that. Do you really want to hurt Randy? No, you don't, you just want him to respect you. So you've got to work it out somehow, to get his respect. But movies that show other ways of resolving conflict aren't exciting. The peaceful hero is seen as a wimp; the violent hero everybody thinks is cool.

"What we need is a Warrior for Peace, someone who is seen as really powerful and brave, but who uses his brain to stop conflict. He may have to fight sometimes but since he's a skilled fighter he'll do less harm than an untrained fighter—he'll know just how much force to use in each situation. Most of your action heroes use extreme force when they could just as easily use little or no force. But in a society where aggressive people always seem to wind up with the most power and money, it's hard to get respect for *peacefully* fighting injustice.

"Do you know what injustice means?" Lamar spoke with feeling, "It means not acting fair. Like treating people who seem different unfairly, maybe because of the color of their skin, or a physical handicap, or because they come from another country, or even kids like you who get bullied here at school just because you're a good student. That's prejudice. That's what creates violence."

"Whatever the reason, I hate being picked on," Henry responded to what Lamar was saying. "But I know what you mean about too much violence. It's like all those schools where shootings happened—some kids just lose it. They get revenge on the bullies but kill a lot of innocent people as well. That's really terrible. I remember one kid saying on TV that if you push people like him they push back. I felt sorry for him and the people he hurt.

"So what can I do about it? If you hadn't come along those bullies would have just beaten me up like they always do. You're the first person who ever helped me. The teachers and the principal pretend like they don't see what's really going on. I think they're afraid of the bullies and afraid of what their parents might do if they were kicked out of school. Those guys get away with murder because they're good athletes. I don't think that they would even be punished if they really busted me up. Their parents would probably get lawyers to get them off. I just wish I could get back at them and show them how bad it feels."

"You can beat those bullies by learning the martial arts, martial arts for peace, that is," Lamar interrupted. "I'm not talking about the martial arts you see in those video games with all the blood flying and stuff. And not the martial arts in those stupid action films, which is just more violence. Ever see reruns on TV of that show *Kung Fu?* It's about a kid who grew up in a Chinese temple, like a church, but where they taught martial arts. His teachers called him 'Grasshopper,' but his real name is Kane. When he leaves, he goes to America and wanders around the old West, which was a pretty tough place. Kane knows how to fight but more importantly he has learned how to stop conflict without using force. Except for one time when he killed a bad guy who has just killed his teacher, he stops people from hurting him and other people mostly by nonviolent ways. It's really cool because he's truly a Black Belt Warrior for Peace, someone who's strong and brave and uses physical force only if he has to, if there's no other way. He fights against

18

injustice and helps people like you who are being picked on by bullies. He can do this because he learned special skills to stop bullies from hurting others," Lamar went on in an excited way.

"I wish I could go to that temple or whatever in China and learn what he did," Henry said in a sad tone of voice.

Lamar laughed, "You don't have to go that far, Grasshopper! Look, I'm taking classes at this awesome martial arts school in town. You can go there too. I've been at it awhile, so you wouldn't be in my class, but I'll take you there and introduce you to the head teacher. He's really cool. He'll want to interview you first, though. He doesn't take people unless they're serious. A lot of kids just want to kick butt, or win trophies at tournaments, but what they teach at this place is different. You'll see."

Henry didn't have to think about it for a second. "I suppose I have to ask my mom and dad first," he said, "but I'm ready to start. Wow, thanks!"

Later that week Henry went with Lamar to the martial arts school and began a journey that would change his life for the better.

Martial Arts That Are for Peace

Lamar's martial arts school was in a house on the other side of the city. It was in a nice neighborhood with lots of trees. The house had a large window in front, and in the window was a painting showing a piece of bamboo inside a circle. As they entered the house the first thing Henry saw was an office to the left and some chairs facing a long room straight in front of him. The long room had a clean, bright wooden floor. On a table next to the chairs was a display of books and on the wall there were two posters. One of the posters said "Martial Arts Code of Conduct," and showed people bowing. Written below were things like "Respect is honoring the dignity of all life" and "Kindness is caring for others as you would like to be cared for." Another poster showed a kid being picked on by a bully. At the top were the words, "12 Ways to Defeat the Bully." At the bottom were little boxes with the different ways, such as "Use Humor," "Reason with the Bully," and "Make Friends."

Lamar introduced Henry to an older man dressed in a plain white martial arts uniform. Lamar had told Henry earlier that students called the man Sensei, which roughly means "teacher," but actually was a Japanese word meaning "someone who has gone before."

"Hello, sir," said Henry, all the while gazing at the bully in the poster and thinking about Randy and his gang.

"Are you interested in defeating the bully the smart way?" he asked right off to Henry's surprise. But before Henry could reply, the Sensei said, "I see you're interested in that poster. You know, I was bullied when I was young too." He invited Henry to sit down and with real concern in his voice asked, "Is that why you're here?"

Henry explained his situation at school while the kindly teacher listened carefully. It was the first time that someone really listened to Henry, especially an adult. He could tell that this teacher was interested. After Henry finished, the Sensei reflected a moment, and then spoke:

"You seem like a kind and thoughtful young man, not one who wants to learn martial arts just to get revenge and make himself a big shot. I think that here you can learn how to deal with those bullies and others like them that you will meet in life. But first you must try to understand what we do. Many people think that the martial arts just teach more violence and this is true in too many cases. But what we teach here is different; here we teach a complete conflict education program. We call it A.R.M., 'A' for 'Avoid,' 'R' for 'Resolve,' and 'M' for 'Manage.'

"Before I go any further, I want to tell you something important. What I am telling you now and what you will be learning here, if you want to stay, is not easy to understand at first. It will get easier later, but only after hard work. You must be dedicated. You must be committed. You must practice a lot. You will need to take what you learn here at this martial arts school and try it out in your daily life. It will do you no good to just practice it in here.

"The martial arts we will teach you has to be practical, has to help you every day to resolve conflict, build character, and create peace, not only in your life now, here in this town, but also when you become an adult and go out into the world. Do you understand? And also, you will need to find out for yourself if what we tell you is true. Don't accept it without question. Use that muscle between your ears, your brain. It has to be exercised just like your body. You'll need to keep both fit and healthy. Does this make some sense to you? I know that you are probably just hearing these things for the first time. Have patience. If you don't understand what's being said, then ask. That is your responsibility. And if we are going too fast for you, ask us to slow down and go over things that you're not sure of."

He asked Henry if he had any questions. Henry was a bit overwhelmed by all the Sensei had said so he just answered, "No."

"No, sir, would be a better answer. Please remember that it is important to have the proper manners. Manners are part of the Martial Arts Code of Conduct we will be teaching you. As you will see, acting with good manners actually helps make people feel good. They help smooth things out between people and reduce the chance for conflict. This is our main goal, to help you to understand and resolve conflict peacefully, without the use of force. There may be times when you'll have to protect yourself or other people, but with our training most of the time you'll be able to prevent conflict from happening. Remember, conflict is a part of life. It's what you do about it that counts."

Henry was then invited to stay and observe a class. He was asked to sit in the open area in front of the long wooden floor. Lamar's class wasn't until later, so he sat with Henry. While they were waiting, Lamar showed Henry some of the books on the table. They were about bullying, prejudice, and martial arts for peace. Henry noticed that they were all written by the Sensei.

After a while a group of young people came in, some with their parents and others with friends. They were carrying black bags along with their schoolbooks. They took off their shoes and socks, and with great care placed them on wooden shelves. They then walked along the side of the long room on a long narrow carpet so they didn't have to walk on the wooden floor to get to the changing rooms in back.

After a while they reappeared, filing out in an orderly way and bowing before entering the area with the wooden floor. They were dressed in plain white uniforms with different colored belts tied around their waists. Soon two other adults entered and politely introduced themselves to Henry. They were the older teacher's assistants, Mr. Lee, an Asian-American and Ms. Watts, an African-American.

The class came to order when Ms. Watts asked the students to line up. They lined up in order of rank, with the teachers sitting in front, facing the students. Everyone was quiet for a minute or two; they then bowed to each other respectfully.

Mr. Lee led the class in warm-ups and light stretching. The Sensei and Ms. Watts moved around the students demonstrating the proper way to warm up and stretch. After about fifteen minutes, they all began to practice graceful, dancelike movements. There was no rock and roll music, no saluting, no yelling military commands like Henry had heard they used at martial arts schools. Instead there was a gentle yet firm encouragement from each teacher.

After about half an hour of physical work, the students were asked to sit down in a semicircle. The Sensei opened one of his books and read a story called "Do You Mind If I Warm Up?" It was about a young boy who had successfully avoided a bully for a long time, but was finally cornered by the bully in a dead-end alley. "Now I've got you," yelled the bully. "I'm going to bust you up good."

"I guess you've finally got me cornered, so we'll just have to fight," the young boy replied. "But do you mind if I warm up first?" The bully was so surprised by this request, he didn't say anything. The young man then stepped back and demonstrated his martial art skills, punching and kicking the air with great skill and power. On seeing this show of strength, the bully had second thoughts.

"Aw, I don't have time for you now," he said as he quickly retreated, "but just stay out of my way!"

"Students, what does this real-life story show you about the martial arts?" Sensei asked. "What did the young boy do to defeat the bully the smart way?"

A student with bright red hair responded, "He used the number 12 on the '12 Ways' chart. He stood up to the bully by taking a martial stance and showed the bully what he could do if the bully really wanted to fight. He knew he had the power to win but he also had the skills he needed to walk away with confidence."

"Yes, you are quite right. This story is a good example of a Black Belt Warrior for Peace, a martial artist who had the skill to defend himself physically but used the mental martial arts instead. He realized that a show of force was all that he needed to get this bully to back off. Many people think that all you need is physical self-defense skills to deal with bullies, that to win you must always fight. But we can see from this story that isn't correct; there are other options. We must understand and practice mental self-defense skills along with physical ones so we have a complete martial art practice."

Then, with the help of his assistants, the Sensei divided the students into groups of two. They acted out some roles, one taking the part of the bully and the other the one being picked on. After they did that for a time, they sat again while the Sensei talked about "body language," how your body gives off signals about what you're thinking.

"Students, if you can understand what someone's body language is telling you, you will be able to read the bully's mind. You will be able to stop conflict from happening because you will be aware of the potential for it in the minds of potential bullies even before they are aware of it in themselves," he instructed the students.

Class ended with the practice of "forms," artistic physical movements that didn't look very martial at all. Then the Sensei addressed his students. His tone was serious.

"Like many of you, when I was young I suffered from being bullied. Years later, after I studied the martial arts and then began to teach them, I realized that I had to find a new way to help people resolve conflict peacefully. I knew that meant I had to teach more than physical self-defense skills. I had to create a martial art that would teach treating people with kindness and respect. I wanted to help young people understand and deal with the terrible bullying that comes from prejudice. I knew that the martial arts that I had been taught had to change in order to meet the real needs you young people have every day, in getting along with your parents, friends, and people in your community, not only in your own neighborhood but around the world.

"You are the new generation. You will change the world for the better because you will understand how to resolve conflict peacefully, which is the true intention of all martial arts. That's what this school is about, teaching a martial art that can resolve conflict, build character, and create peace. The world needs help, and learning martial arts for peace is one way you can help.

"I am getting older now. I've been in the martial arts for over forty years. I want to pass on what I know to you so you can carry on and build upon what we've started. You will need courage. You will need to be brave. You will need a strong spirit in order to be a Black Belt Warrior for Peace. The word 'warrior' here means someone who stands up for peace, someone who fights injustice. There are many great modern-day warriors, like Dr. Martin Luther King and Ceasar Chavez, who stood up for justice and equality for all people. They're the real heroes because they are champions of peace, not of war. Even though they may never have studied martial arts, they are true Black Belt Warriors for Peace because they battle the fear and ignorance that causes injustice.

"A Black Belt Warrior for Peace is not warlike. A Black Belt Warrior for Peace is bold, determined, and courageous in standing up for what is right. In order for you to become a Black Belt Warrior for Peace you will need many skills for fighting injustice. Perhaps the most important is intelligence, understanding what prevents peace, that is, what creates conflict. You will need these skills to pass the test of conquering fear and ignorance, for it is fear and ignorance that create conflict between people. The truth will free you from fear, and understanding will protect you from ignorance. If you pass, you will have the honor and respect that comes with wearing the Black Belt of a Warrior for Peace."

The class sat in silence for a few minutes. They then bowed to each other in unison and calmly filed off the wooden floor to change back into their street clothes. After class the Sensei thanked Henry for staying to watch.

"You can see that we cover a lot in each class," he said, "Students are expected to learn both physical and mental martial arts skills. They are tested on both for every belt rank advancement. This isn't easy, as you will see. If you want to come back it's your choice. I won't try to convince you to join. It's up to you to choose freely. If you're not ready to make that choice, you're welcome to watch more classes."

"Thank you, sir, for allowing me to watch," Henry replied. "I would really like to take classes." The very next week, after getting his parents' permission and having them also watch a class and meet with the Sensei, Henry started.

The Martial Arts Code of Conduct is the foundation

of all Martial Arts that are for peace. And like a

foundation of a house, the Martial Arts Code of Conduct

is what we build everything on.

The Martial Arts
Code of Conduct

1 Courtesy

Being Well-Mannered and Considerate

It was storming when Henry entered the martial arts school on his first day. He was naturally a bit nervous, but it was warm and inviting inside. He noticed the smell of sweat and floor polish. Sensei introduced Henry to the rest of the students at the start of class. Henry was wearing his new uniform with a white belt tied around his waist. It felt stiff and strange, and he wasn't used to going barefoot. He lined up following the directions of Ms. Watts. A higher-level student was assigned to stand next to Henry and help him get used to the new routine.

"We're going to review the first point of the Martial Arts Code of Conduct, especially for the new students," Sensei announced. "We go over this many times because you can always learn something new. The Martial Arts Code of Conduct is the foundation of this school and all martial arts that are for peace. And like a foundation of a house, the Martial Arts Code of Conduct is what we build everything on. This is what you must master if you want to be a Black Belt Warrior for Peace. To be a 'master' you have to develop your skills to a high degree. And this goes on your whole life. There is no magical stopping point when you've arrived. So, who knows what is first in the Martial Arts Code of Conduct?"

A slim girl with long hair raised her hand. "Courtesy," she called out.

"That's right, courtesy. Courtesy is being well-mannered and considerate. But rather than just talk about it, let's try a little experiment. Remember I told you that what we teach you here must be applied to your daily life, or it will be of no value? So I'd like you to go home tonight and after dinner when your parents tell you to do the dishes, or your homework, don't argue or resist. Instead, get up from the table and bow and say 'Thank you.' And then do what they ask without any complaint. At your next class tell us what happened."

For the rest of the class time that day the students worked on what they called "basics." The basics meant first having a strong and proper stance.

"The stance is the foundation of your art," Mr. Lee told the class. "Everything is built on the stance, so learn it well."

The class was also shown what goes into a single martial arts movement, like a block or punch. Sensei had written up a seven-page outline showing all that went into that one movement.

"That's why a martial arts punch is just not a regular punch. The martial arts punch is very powerful because so much goes into it," Mr. Lee went on instructing the class. "But again let me remind you that there are two different but similar parts of the martial arts. One is the 'martial' part, the practical, physical, self-defense skills you need to protect yourself. The other part is the 'art' of the martial art. This is what is missing from most martial arts schools. They think that the martial arts are mostly 'martial,' so their places are more like a martial arts 'gym,' where students just hang out and spar with each other just like any boxer or wrestler would do.

"The art of the martial arts is to take you beyond yourself. The punch then is not a punch but a means of forgetting yourself. When you are so focused on that single movement, when you give your total attention to that punch, then there is no violence. The punch then becomes a way of peace. You may not be able to understand what I'm saying until you experience it. A similar feeling you might have had is when you ride your bike down a hill and you're going too fast. There's a moment when you may feel out of control because you're going too fast. But then you let go and it feels like you're free, like

you're flying. At that moment you're beyond yourself, beyond your fear. It's the same with the 'art' of punching. You go beyond yourself, beyond fear and anger, and because you do you're free. In that space free of fear there is no violence; in fact, quite the opposite, you feel really at peace.

"Most people who practice the martial arts never get to understand this. They may feel it at certain times but because their teacher hasn't pointed it out and discussed it, they will probably just think it is some nice feeling but with no real meaning. But this feeling and its meaning are the reason we study the martial arts in the first place. It's the most important thing the martial arts can teach us because it's what can bring an end to conflict between people.

"Conflict is created by fear, which is part of ourselves. And when we go beyond ourselves, like when you are speeding down that steep hill on your bike, we go beyond fear. Just for that moment. Sometimes that moment feels so good we try to get it again but then what we get is not that *true* feeling but just a *thought* about that feeling. The true feeling can only come when we don't try to get it directly. It only comes when we don't expect it.

"If after feeling that free moment of going beyond yourself you go to the top of the hill and try to recapture it, what you will get will not be the same. But through the 'art' of the martial arts, you can discover a way to recapture this feeling. The way is both very simple and also very hard—you have to train hard and work on your form. Your form is how well you do a technique. This is why Sensei wrote this seven-page outline about what goes into a single martial arts move like a punch. He's giving us a 'map' so that we can create the right foundation—like an invitation for that feeling to happen again. There is nothing else you can do except to practice your form over and over and over so that it seems to happen by itself. If you practice your form in this way then the form takes over at some point without you ever really being aware of it. It's like wearing a suit of clothes that you never take off. At some point it becomes as natural as your own skin.

"This is why we encourage you to keep on practicing one technique, like a punch, over and over, until you're completely tired of it, and then we push you to practice it even more. It's at that point, when you go beyond your exhaustion that the feeling may happen again. But remember this also means we are teaching you about understanding yourself and how conflict is created. So we are preparing you mentally as well as physically. The mental preparation is just as important as the physical.

"Most martial arts teachers make you practice physical skills over and over and nothing else. Maybe this is because their teacher taught that way, and their teacher's teacher before that did also, going back for hundreds of years. And since it has been done this way for so long they just do it without really knowing why. This they call 'tradition.'

"Or some teachers will reject tradition because they don't understand why they have to repeat these moves over and over. So they make the martial art 'modern' and throw out all the tradition. Then their school looks more like a gym, with classes being offered in martial arts aerobics or some popular fitness fad with a martial arts touch. This is sad because they have then lost the real essence of the martial arts, the art of 'empty self,' which is what martial arts are truly all about. The 'art' of any martial art is as important as the 'martial,' because it is what allows you to go beyond yourself, to go beyond the fear. Unfortunately this idea, this balance, has for the most part been lost. But here at this school we're aware of its importance even though it might not be popular. What is good for you and good for martial arts is not entertainment—it won't make an exciting movie.

"Now these are difficult subjects and I know that you newcomers may be a bit confused about what I am saying. But you cannot expect to understand it right away, just as you cannot expect to earn a black belt in a day. It takes years of hard training, both mentally and physically. There is no instant success like they often say in ads. You get out of the martial arts what you put into it. It's entirely up to you. But we at least want you to know that there are these two different yet similar parts of the martial arts so you can begin to think about it as we go through our classes together. If we don't at least try to explain it to you , you may just get tired of how we are teaching you and leave. There are many martial arts schools out there that will use all kinds of ways to get you to belong, some of which are not right."

The class ended with the students again practicing their forms, this time, Henry sensed, with a little more feeling than before. Before leaving to change clothes they all lined up and bowed again.

"Now don't forget about your test of bowing tonight," Mr. Lee reminded them. "And remember what happens. You should find it interesting, and we will discuss it in our next class."

Later that evening Henry tried out the bowing experiment that his teacher asked the students to do. Just as they were finishing dinner, Henry's mother asked him to do the dishes in a rather sarcastic way, as if she expected Henry to resist.

"Henry, just this once, do you suppose you could do the dishes without complaining?"

Henry quickly got up from the table and bowed. "Yes, Mother. Thank you. I'll be glad to help by doing the dishes," he added for an extra touch.

Henry's mother stood there with her mouth open staring in disbelief at her son. "Glad to do the dishes?" she stammered. "Henry, is something wrong?"

"Not at all. It will be my pleasure to do the dishes," Henry said trying to conceal the smile creeping across his face. He scooped up a stack of dirty dishes and went off to the kitchen, leaving his parents silently sitting in wonder at the dining room table.

The next class Henry couldn't wait to hear what the other students had to say about their assignment of bowing. Finally, at the end of the class, Ms. Watts asked them to share their stories. Some told stories similar to Henry's, at which everyone had a good laugh. Then one of the younger kids spoke.

"I did what you told me to and an amazing thing happened," he said shyly. "When I bowed and said I would do what my parents asked, my mother almost fainted!" The whole class had a really good laugh at that.

"The first principle in the Martial Arts Code of Conduct is courtesy, being well-mannered and considerate. To be considerate means to show respect for others. This is the first step in preventing conflict," Sensei stated. "Can you tell me about bad manners? Give me some examples. You don't have to mention names, just your experiences."

"I don't like it when my sister eats with her mouth full. It's gross to see the food half eaten in her mouth. And it makes such gross noises," one of the younger students spoke up. "I also don't like it when my sister talks on the phone all night. She tells me to get out of her room when I try to tell her that I need to use the phone," he continued.

Another girl spoke up, "It really bothers me when my friends say bad things about other kids in the class behind their backs. I mean, everyone in my class knows each other, and my friends would never say anything mean to someone to their face. But the minute we're talking by ourselves they start criticizing some of the other kids. It really makes me uncomfortable."

"Well, some people could use a little criticism," said the boy next to her. "Kids in my school cut in line in the cafeteria. Then they mess the tables up with food and garbage and just leave it for others to clean up."

"I think bad manners are when people ask you questions and don't even bother to listen to your answers," said another boy. "Like every day my dad asks, 'How was school today?' and while I'm telling him what I did and everything, he's just staring at the TV or the newspaper."

"I think that bad manners are when people cut in front of your car just to get ahead, or to beat the light. It seems crazy out there on the highways with everybody going so fast. It's scary. Everybody's so rude to each other they get into fights because of 'road rage,'" another student spoke up.

The students gave many examples of bad manners, some funny and others dangerous.

"So if we all know that these are bad manners, why do people keep on doing these things?" Sensei asked the students. "Is it because manners were not taught them when they were young? Or is it because many people think that manners are just silly rules that they don't have to obey? Whatever the reason, you can see from all these examples how much conflict and irritation bad manners can cause. It may seem funny when someone answers the phone with a grumpy voice, but it's not so funny when 'road rage' leads to an auto accident. So you can see how important it is to have good manners. It's like your stances in the martial arts. A proper stance gives you a strong foundation for your physical techniques. Manners are the proper foundation for people getting along. They help prevent conflict, which is the basic intention of all martial arts.

"Let's finish the class with a period of quiet," Sensei suggested. "Let's spend the next three minutes thinking about our own bad manners. Are we guilty of doing any of those things that we've said are bad manners? What can we do or stop doing that will cause a little less stress and irritation to our parents or teachers or friends? If we each make one improvement in our manners, the world will be just a little bit better."

The class ended with three minutes of quiet. Henry resolved not to argue or complain whenever he was asked to do the dishes. And, funny thing, he felt good about his resolution.

Gentleness

Living with Affection and Compassion

2

For weeks Henry and the class worked very hard on their basics. Henry felt a bit clumsy, especially when he watched more advanced students practice their forms so skillfully. Henry didn't think it looked violent at all, yet he knew it wasn't dancing. It was hard to describe, seeming both powerful and beautiful at the same time.

Today was the first time Henry had ever practiced self-defense. It felt good to begin learning how to protect himself. He knew that he didn't want to really hurt anyone, and was glad to see that some of the techniques were simply ways to escape from a bully's grasp and get away. Others required skills he wasn't used to. Some of the techniques made his stomach knot up because he sensed what they could do to a person.

"If you feel confident that you know how to protect yourself because you have learned self-defense techniques then you won't panic when a bully approaches you. This confidence allows you to use your first two lines of defense, to avoid and then, if necessary, to resolve conflict peacefully, without the use of physical force. It's really that simple," Mr. Lee instructed.

"But in learning self-defense you need to know how to respond at the right level with the right technique. If a bully just says 'Give me your lunch money!' what do you think is the proper response?" he asked.

A senior student answered, "I'd first use my mental martial arts and choose one of the '12 Ways,' maybe using humor. If I could get him to laugh at a joke, then maybe I could talk to him and make friends."

"Yes, that would be a good choice," Mr. Lee replied. "Using mental self-defense is the best thing to do. But what if the bully grabs you by the shirt? Would you kick him? Would you punch him in the face with the possibility of breaking his nose? Or would that be too much? Has anyone heard that expression 'Let the punishment fit the crime'? Do you know what it means?"

"Doing to the bully what he is doing to you?" asked another student.

"Well, sort of. That's close. Think about it some more," Mr. Lee encouraged them.

"I think it means that if the bully only grabs you, you should try to use a self-defense technique that is best for that level," another student replied. "Kicking or punching at this stage wouldn't be right. He isn't really hurting you so you can use a simple release technique and then get out of there instead of starting right in fighting."

"That's true. But what if the bully does start to punch you? Should you punch or kick him then?" Mr. Lee followed up.

"No, because the same rule applies. You can block the punch. We've been taught that the martial arts is self-defense, not offense. We've practiced a blocking-only pattern that lets us avoid having to strike first. And we've learned other ways to avoid a punch, like ducking or stepping out of the way into a back stance."

"Then 'letting the punishment fit the crime' really means responding with a technique appropriate to the bully's action. If you litter, or cross the street against the traffic light, a policeman might give you a ticket, and maybe you'll have to pay a fine. But he won't throw you in jail. If he did you'd feel you were treated unfairly and probably lose respect for the law. You might even want to get back at him somehow. It's the same with a physical confrontation; you should respond with an action that is appropriate for what the other person is doing to you. If you go beyond that, the violence will escalate.

"The 'Target' poster here shows you the right level of response for the level of attack. It's the '12 Ways to Defeat the Bully' that you're already familiar with, but broken up into three columns with four ways in each column. Some of you call these columns, 'mild, medium, and hot,' like salsa. That's a good way to consider your mental martial arts and

the physical self-dense skills as well. Each level of attack should be met with the same level of defense. There's no need for overdoing it. That's why a trained martial artist will do less harm than an untrained person. The untrained person will strike out with too much uncontrolled power, which could really hurt another person and probably isn't needed. A trained fighter will know how to apply the right technique to a particular level of threat and so harm less, especially when he or she has many skills to draw from. Of course it is best to avoid a fight by using your head instead of your fists. Using the '12 Ways' is really very important. But even more important is understanding and avoiding conflict before it happens. Knowing how to avoid, resolve, and manage conflict are all a part of the Martial Arts Code of Conduct.

"Today," he went on, "we are going to talk about gentleness, living with affection and compassion. Do you know what compassion means?"

"Doesn't it mean to feel sorry for someone?" one of the younger students asked.

"That's close. Would someone get the dictionary from the resource table and bring it over here? Thanks. Remember, if you don't know what a word means, you should look it up in a dictionary. It's your responsibility to educate yourself too. Learning together here is a partnership, which means that all of us, students and teachers, are working and learning together. Will one of you read the definition?"

"Compassion," a student read loudly, "a feeling of sorrow or pity for the sufferings and misfortunes of others; sympathy."

"It doesn't say who we should have sympathy for," Mr. Lee observed. "Can we have compassion for a bully?"

"Not me," Henry suddenly heard himself say. Several students turned to look at him. "I mean, I was pushed around by some big kids," Henry explained, "and believe me, I'm the one that was in pain. They weren't hurting, so I don't know why I should feel sorry for them."

"Are you sure?" asked Mr. Lee. "Or has a bully suffered because she or he was picked on too? Isn't that possible?"

Henry thought a moment, but didn't have a reply.

"In some of our classes coming up," Mr. Lee continued, "we'll each have a chance to play the part of the bully, so we can get to know how the bully feels. It's like getting into the bully's shoes and walking around in them for awhile. I think you'll begin to understand then that most bullies do what they do because someone has bullied them. When we understand that the bully has been hurt too, we can have compassion."

"How many other people here have been bullied?" Mr. Lee asked in response to Henry's statement. Nearly everyone in the class held a hand up. "Perhaps some of you would like to share your own stories of being bullied?"

A small redheaded boy wearing glasses said with feeling, "I remember being held down by two bullies while another one beat up my friend. And I couldn't do anything! I felt so angry but I didn't want to cry and show them that I was afraid. It happened to me in the second grade. The same bullies would take my glasses and throw them in the toilet or they would smack me with wet towels in the locker room after gym class."

"They called me fat and a nerd. Then they tore up my homework and threw it down the sewer," another student responded.

"I was beaten up so badly that I had to go to the hospital," said a tall, slim student named Owen, who usually didn't say much. "I bashed my head on the curb when the bully knocked me over with my own bike after he took it from me. The doctor told me when he was stitching me up that if the wound had been closer to my temple I could have died. I was so bummed out, because I didn't have a bike all summer. And I was angry, at the bully, sure, but at everybody because they just said 'Forget about it.'

"But one day Sensei and I had a long talk about it. He told me he was bullied when he was a kid. I was amazed. Anyway, he helped me get over my anger and depression by showing me that even though it was the bully who first hurt me, by holding onto my anger I was hurting myself. I'm not sure I believed him then, but I kept practicing my mental and physical martial arts skills. And one day, just strolling down the street, I saw him, the bully, standing on the front porch of a house. I stopped and he gave me a kind of funny stare, and we stood there like that for a few moments when all of a sudden I realized that I wasn't afraid anymore. And I think he knew it.

"Anyway, just as I was thinking, 'If he tries anything now, I can whip him,' all of a sudden this big fat guy, his dad I guess, came out of the house and started yelling at him and smacking him around. What a beating! Boy, I felt sorry for the guy.

"Looking back now I know that he must have been smacked around by his dad and who knows who else. When he took my bike and knocked me down he was probably just as angry and unhappy as I was. It's funny, I still see him around, but now I think he knows that I am different. I don't feel or act like a victim anymore but, you know, he still does."

The class fell quiet after this long story. It seemed to Henry that everyone was thinking about the kids who bullied them and wondering whether they had also been bullied. Henry had thought that maybe he was the only one who had suffered from bullying. It helped him a lot to hear all the stories.

Mr. Lee broke into their thoughts, "So can you understand that bullies were taught to be bullies because they were bullied themselves? Can you begin to feel compassion for them? Maybe it's hard at first because the hurt is still too fresh, too strong. Maybe not the physical hurt but the emotional one. Those scars last far longer than the physical ones. I think that everyone gets bullied, some worse than others. And I think that most people, in some way, can be bullies too. It's what we do about it that counts.

"Conflict is part of life. If we want to get help we can. But we must be willing to find out where and how and then work at it. I can't emphasize enough that it takes work to do this, but I can also promise you that it's worthwhile. It is work that brings a great reward, that of growing up and being able to face the challenges of life more intelligently. Ignorance is not bliss. Ignorance is just ignoring, and ignoring bullying allows our fear and unhappiness to grow. And that's not healthy for us.

"Remember to take what you learned here and apply it to your daily life," Mr. Lee said gently. "It's up to you."

While lying awake in his bed that night Henry thought about what he had heard in class. He thought about Randy, and Tyler, and Jake, and whether they had ever been bullied. Was it possible? Was it possible that they had even felt as helpless and angry as Henry had?

Outside his window there was a full moon. And the night sky seemed endless. He fell asleep with a calmer spirit than he had in many weeks.

Honesty

Being Truthful

One day while waiting for his martial arts class to begin, Henry sat reading a martial arts magazine that a friend had given him. On the cover were two men in colorful martial arts uniforms. One was making a terrible face while at the same time kicking the man behind him in the stomach. The man being kicked was flying backwards, looking very shocked. Inside the magazine were lots of photos of martial artists fighting, with stories describing how powerful and deadly their arts and techniques were. One story bragged that you could defeat anyone with a special two-inch power punch that could send an opponent flying. Another showed a small man in a fancy gold uniform with lots of patches throwing another man through the air without even touching him.

Some pictures Henry found really unbelievable. One showed a fierce-looking man dressed in a martial arts uniform that looked liked the American flag—red, white, and blue, with stars and stripes. With one hand he was smashing a pile of flaming cinder blocks while with the other he was smashing a stack of three-hundred-pound blocks of ice. The title of the story read, "Great Grand Master Oleg Grigovich, 10th Degree Black Belt in a dozen different martial arts, beats world record in breaking." The story went on to offer his amazing black belt course for only $49 , guaranteed to make you an honorary master of the Ninja Death Touch Art in thirty days or your money back.

pionship block breakers
ets of fire and ice
f strength.

ivkalzpzppapoidks
:ucvsl dlkd lck sljg-
vlv;alakjlkjaljkdlkjdl
e;oiujh[do/l;sedkjv
aldljalkblkasalkj
ngujzdvin
nag[ojn
kj;lkd
jdllkja
l;lkjd;lkd;l

:lkal;kd
kjd;lkak
jd;lkjlka
l;ljf;lkja
;lka;lk
/l;lkvdlkj
;f;lkjd;lka
;lkdflklsl
a;lkj
aslkja f-0d-= kjd dlak f0e9
aj;lkd
kdlia;lkd

Another article was about a woman grand master who was pictured in long fancy robes with a lot of bare-chested men in martial arts pants standing around her. She was shooting water at them through a fire hose. She called this a "Cleansing Ceremony." Another photo in the same article showed her flying through the air over the heads of her students, about ten feet above the ground.

There were also ads for "special forces" and "foreign military martial arts" that you could learn by ordering some books or attending workshops. It didn't say how much the workshops cost; a number to call was given. An ad that particularly caught Henry's attention promised to teach you how to fight like a bouncer in a bar. It showed a man in regular clothes staring out of the pages right at you. Henry was startled by the look in his eyes, a mixture of intense rage and fear. It reminded him of the faces of Randy, Tyler, and Jake when they picked on him. Engrossed in the magazine, Henry hadn't noticed Mr. Lee, who had been looking at the magazine over his shoulder.

"Pretty amazing stuff," Mr. Lee commented. "It doesn't seem much like that we teach here, does it?"

"I guess not," said Henry, "but it reminds me of another school my mom took me to a few years ago, after some bully gave me a black eye."

"Tell me about it," invited Mr. Lee.

"I remember it was in a shopping mall," Henry recalled. "The teacher was maybe only in his twenties but my mom had to call him 'grand master.' His uniform reminded me of the ones in this magazine. It was purple and white and had a lot of fancy patches. On the back was his name and the word 'Romantique,' which I thought was weird for the name for a martial arts school. Mom told me later it was the name of a company that made hair spray and stuff like that. She said some people get paid by companies to promote their products, like the sports stars on TV. I guess they get a lot of money for wearing those company patches on their uniforms.

"The grand master took my mom and me into his office and he really turned it on. He said that his style of martial arts was the best, and that he came from a long line of great grand masters. He said that I would be guaranteed to be successful in life if I studied with him. His voice really got kind of crazy. He kept telling me to stand up straight and look him right in the eyes and say, 'Yes, Master,' every time he asked me a question.

He put his face right up to mine. His eyes looked a little weird. He kept asking me if I wanted to be a failure or a success in life. I just wanted to get out of there.

"After that we watched a class. The grand master was busy on his cell phone all the time while another teacher, who looked about sixteen, ran the class. One funny thing I remember was the teacher's black belt; it was so long that it almost touched the floor. It was real wide and had lots of gold writing all over it.

"On one wall were some foreign flags over a picture of some old Asian-looking guy with a long beard. The students all lined up and did some weird saluting to the wall. They played some strange foreign music when they did this, and seemed to take the whole thing very seriously. On another wall were a bunch of photos of famous action film stars shaking hands with the master.

"The little kids were funny," Henry smiled. "Some were so small they could hardly walk, but they were called the Tiny Dragons or something. A couple of them didn't want to leave their moms because they were afraid. The older kids were called the Ninja Warriors. Some of them really got into it. They acted really fierce, shouting and making faces. They all practiced a lot of punching and kicking some bags around the room. The bags were life-size and were painted with bully-like kid faces, but had no arms. The little kids were really beating them up. They seemed to really get a thrill out of performing. They looked like those kids you see in the martial arts movies, like Hollywood actors. They didn't seem real. And they played rock music when they practiced!

"At that school the kids practiced a lot of weapons," Henry went on. "There were lots of them hanging on the walls, all kinds of swords, spears, long wooden sticks with chains, and even small knives and cutting things. At first I thought it was cool but after thinking about it, it scared me a little. I mean, what are they doing with all these weapons? Will I have to use them? Later when I thought about it, it seemed pretty silly. What was I going to do, carry a spear to school in case I saw that bully?

"Anyway, I didn't like that school, so when my mom said later that wasn't the right place for me I was really relieved. At first I thought she was just upset because of the weapons. But later, when I heard her talking to dad, she sounded angry. She called the grand master a 'pip-squeak,' and said that he had some nerve, trying to get us both to sign up for two years worth of classes, and no money back if we decided to leave. And

we would be failures in life if we didn't join. She said, 'Who does he think he is?'"

"I see then that you've already been introduced to the 'Take Your Dough' school of martial arts." Mr. Lee smiled at Henry's story. "Your mother is a smart woman."

"You have to watch out for those ridiculous claims, whether in the mall or the magazine," he continued. "There are plenty of false teachers out there, people just in it for a buck. But Henry, there are lots of dishonest people out there in all walks of life. One of the challenges we all have to face in life is to learn to tell the difference between what's honest and dishonest, what's real what's fake, what's important and what's not.

"If someone were to ask me what the secret of life was, I'd probably say 'to enjoy its beauty.'" Mr. Lee went on. "But human beings are too busy and distracted; we've been conditioned to think only about ourselves and our little groups, so we've made a mess of our lives. Our challenge is to understand how we got so messed up and to watch out for the traps of our selfishness and our self-centeredness. You might think it strange when I tell you that this is part of the martial arts. Real martial arts are not just the skills of self-defense but the ability to look at the true and the false and know the difference.

"The real challenge is to be honest in a world that has a lot of dishonesty. I'm not blaming anyone for the way the world is; blame doesn't do any good. I'm just saying it's up to the adults to help young people understand themselves and life in general. I personally think the martial arts school is the perfect place to do this because the martial arts were started by people who wanted not only to protect themselves and have a good physical workout but more importantly to understand themselves. They wanted to know why there was so much suffering in the world, why there was so much conflict and violence. Sure, the martial arts can be put to military and aggressive uses, but those are the wrong, dishonest uses. The martial arts were originally created for the purpose of self-understanding, not war."

"It's hard to be honest," Henry said. "Everyone tells you to tell the truth, that lying is bad, so you're bad if you lie. I used to believe that, because I was afraid: I didn't want to be punished or to feel bad for lying. But as I got older I began to see that people were saying one thing and doing another. I saw lots of adults telling kids to be honest, not to lie or take advantage of other people, but then turning around and being dishonest and lying themselves. I don't get it. It doesn't seem fair."

"I understand how you feel. I was told the same thing when I was a kid, and also began to discover that lots of people weren't doing what they were telling me to. They were 'hypocrites.' That means people who pretend to be something they're not. In other words, someone who says one thing and does something else. I've seen a lot of people in business, especially in the business of the martial arts, who are unethical, dishonest. They don't seem to have any values. They don't have any real morals, any 'Code of Conduct' like we teach here.

"When I was young I was taught, just like you, that I would be punished if I didn't act properly. I wasn't so sure that dishonesty was bad as much as I was *afraid* to be dishonest. But I didn't like feeling that way so I rebelled. I was in trouble a lot. As I got older though, I discovered that I really *wanted* to be good and honest. For one thing, it just naturally felt good to treat others with kindness and courtesy. I also liked it when other people treated me kindly in return. I liked it when they were honest with me. I liked it when they were helpful when I needed help. So I just started to be 'moral' without any pressure to be good. It just came about naturally. But then when I became a martial arts educator—which is what we like to call ourselves to show how we're different from the kind of 'grand master' you met before—I wondered how I was going to teach these morals, these helpful values, to my students.

"What I found out, with Sensei's help, was that I could teach values without putting pressure on the students. I could set up 'tests' that students could use to find out for themselves why it is important to act honestly and kindly. You remember what happened when you cheerfully agreed to do the dishes after dinner? That was one of the tests. This is why it is important to have our Code of Conduct, so students have some sort of 'map' that they can use to find their way in a world that all too often lacks good values. The 'Code of Conduct' I was taught when I was young was based on punishment and reward, which just created conflict in me. The code we have created here includes the same values, but is simply taught in a completely different way. We don't force our values on you. We don't have to, because they're not 'our' values or 'your' values, but rather universal, human values. They belong to no one but can be used by anyone to create harmony and peace.

"It's really quite simple: if your good conduct—your kindness and honesty— is based on fear, sooner or later you will rebel; however, if you discover for yourself the great benefits of kindness and honesty, you will treasure those values and always act in accordance with them. Anyhow, that's why we have a Martial Arts Code of Conduct that's not based on punishments and rewards. Ours is based on understanding, on experiencing what it feels like to be naturally good, honest and kind.

"I hope that I haven't confused you. But it's like Sensei told you when you first came here, it takes time and effort to understand these things. A lot of martial arts schools want to 'dumb it down,' to make it real simple, like what they called on TV 'sound bites.' They make wild claims like 'Seven Lessons for Martial Arts Mastery' or 'How to Be a Black Belt in Business.' They sound appealing but are really a bunch of nonsense. There's no shortcut to success; in fact, there's really no success, because there's always room for improvement."

"I don't mean to be disrespectful, Mr. Lee," said Henry, "but that school I went to had a lot more students than here. If all you say is true, how come more people don't come to learn?"

"That's a good question," Mr. Lee smiled, "and I'm glad you feel comfortable asking it. Asking questions is the best way to find out for yourself what's true and what's not. The truth is that most people want the shortcut. The rewards, like being rich and famous, seem to come not from understanding and being yourself, but by choosing a role in life—doctor, lawyer, businessman—and playing it. They don't think about what would truly make themselves happy, but only about what will impress other people. They do what I call 'fake it, until you make it.' Plus people today have been conditioned to think that you don't have to really work for what you get. What we teach here—good values, self-understanding, and why there is so much suffering and conflict—take a lot longer. However, the teachers here all believe that these can be learned by anyone who wants to take the time and effort. And Sensei has spent his entire life teaching people how."

"I read the Sensei's first book and it was awesome!" Henry said with enthusiasm. "It's true that I had to work at it. I sometimes had to ask my mom just what he was saying. But I like it that he doesn't talk down to me. Do a lot of people read his books?"

"Sure, many people, mainly young people, although he writes some books for adults as well. But he feels strongly that you should learn these things while you're young even though much of what he says may at first be over your head. But with time and patience, two very important things to remember, you'll come to understand what he's saying. That's because it's true, it's real. I don't mean that you have to accept what it says. You should question it to find out for yourself what is true and what is not. He is not asking you to accept *his* truth, or even *his* opinion. He just says this is so. It's up to you to find out if it is true or not" Mr. Lee continued.

"Do people ever disagree with him?" Henry inquired.

"What is honest and true is not something you can agree or disagree about. It is not an opinion. An opinion is your particular feeling about something. For example, if I say strawberry ice cream tastes bad, that would be my opinion, based on what I like or dislike. If you happen to like strawberry ice cream, you can disagree with me, or if you don't like it either, we can agree. In the case of our likes or dislikes about ice cream, we are just offering our opinions. But if I say that ice cream is made from cream, sugar, and a particular flavoring like strawberry or chocolate then I am stating a fact. It is true and I am being honest about it. I am telling you exactly what makes it up. I'm not trying to say ice cream has things in it that it doesn't. What Sensei writes in his books is also based on fact, on scientific observation. He is not asking you to agree or disagree with him. He is not important. But what he is pointing to is. Do you see the difference?"

"Yes, I do," Henry replied.

"You know, since we're talking about honesty, let me tell you that people have stolen Sensei's work and dumbed it down and claimed that it was their own. They didn't even give him credit for it. Not that anyone can own the truth. Facts are facts, but to take a man's life's work in the particular way he has presented it and just steal it is dishonest. The worst thing is that when it is reduced to a simplified form it loses its truth, its real value."

"Why doesn't Sensei do something?" asked Henry. "Can't he sue them?"

"He could, of course," said Mr. Lee, "but he feels that suing is not the answer. There are too many lawyers suing about too many things, and it just hurts the country. There is so much dishonesty that everyone feels like a victim. But rather than talk things out plainly and honestly, they run to lawyers, who don't care as much about putting the matter right as they do getting some money out of it.

"People today more than ever respect wealth, assuming it is the result of hard work. But that is so often not the case." Mr. Lee went on. "Riches quite often come through simple dishonesty and greed. And so many people think, 'Why not, why shouldn't I take all I can get?' without realizing that when they take too much there is little left for others. It's like ordering a pizza for eight people. The pizza has eight pieces. If the first person to help himself takes four pieces, way too much for himself, what's left for the rest? And if the next person takes two pieces and so on, what happens? People act like there is an endless supply of everything, but that isn't true. Many things, especially our natural resources, are running out. But people keep on grabbing whatever they can, assuming it is just their fair share. Even with all the scientific reports telling us of the dangers of our wasteful ways, we rush ahead and consume whatever we want.

"You may wonder what all this has to do with the martial arts. In fact, it relates strongly: The world is in trouble and you have inherited the challenge of righting all these wrongs. You will definitely need a Code of Conduct to guide you. Moreover, the martial arts that are for peace—not those only interested in competition or physical fitness—are concerned with the world. Remember, the main goal of all martial arts that are for peace is to understand and stop conflict.

"We feel that with the right understanding and hard work we can turn this greed and dishonesty around. It is resolvable. Everything we do affects the world and everybody in it, for better or worse. We are the world and the world is us. Every one of us martial arts educators believes in this, some more, perhaps some less. But it is the most important thing we can teach you so that you can live on this beautiful earth in peace and contentment.

"It's in your hands. With the right education you can make a difference. That's what martial arts that are for peace are about. When you first came here you probably thought that martial arts for peace were just punching and kicking. Now you know they're about understanding yourself and the world. Are you ready for that?"

Humility

Acting Without Self-Importance

4

Some of the senior students at Henry's martial arts school were participating in a local martial arts competition and all the students were invited to attend. Henry had never been to a martial arts tournament. It was held in a large building in a convention center, and there were hundreds of kids with their instructors there, from schools all over the state. The kids from Henry's school sat with Ms. Watts and Mr. Lee in a special area reserved for them.

Sensei had talked in class about what he thought a good tournament should be like. He felt that the skill of the contestant needed to be tested. The problem with many tournaments, he had said, was that the desire to win at all costs emphasized the individual over everyone else. He felt that a sense of cooperative competition was what was missing. By cooperative competition he meant that the participants should work together to help each other develop better skills. The goal was not winning but testing your opponent's skills. If each contestant did his or her best the result would be that both would improve. There were no real winners or losers. Sensei called it a "win-win" situation for everyone.

Sensei believed that it was important that this attitude of competitive cooperation be brought into the daily lives of the students, so they could work together at school, at home, and in the community to help each other be the best they could be. They wouldn't be trying to *beat* each other, so much as *challenge* each other to grow and learn for the betterment of all.

"There are different schools of thought about competition and different kinds of tournaments," Mr. Lee spoke to the students around him as they sat waiting for the tournament to start. "Sensei talked to you about one difference, between competition and cooperative competition, where everyone wins by helping each other to be better. There is also another difference that I think is important for you to understand. I guess you could put it simply by saying there is the school of full contact and the school of full power. I think that watching today's tournament will help you understand the difference, because today is a full-contact event.

"They call it 'sparring,' like when you practice boxing with a partner at a boxing gym. When I was first learning the martial arts, we called it *kumite*, a Japanese word that describes something very different from what you'll see here. It's also called 'freestyle,' which means that it isn't 'fixed.' Fixed style means that you practice particular self-defense techniques with a partner—you each perform certain prearranged movements to attack and defend. This improves timing and coordination. With either fixed or freestyle you can practice what is called 'responsing,' which means that you move exactly like your partner is moving, like being a shadow. But more than just copying your partner's moves, you practice to become sensitive to your partner's state of mind, so you can anticipate his or her next move and move just before it. You 'intuit,' which means you become aware of a 'feeling' that comes from your partner, and you immediately act on that. It's difficult to understand until you actually do it. Most people have this ability naturally but they're not aware of it and don't practice it.

"Have you ever gone into a place and felt uncomfortable, like when you feel there is something wrong but you can't quite put it into words what it is? But you feel something bad, so strongly that you want to get out of there? This is what I'm talking about. Practicing 'responsing' helps you to be more aware, more sensitive to things at this 'feeling' level. It helps you to sense danger and act on it quickly before anything really bad happens.

"The full contact we see here is sparring. It's based on points that the judges award you when you hit your opponent in a potentially harmful way, which really just means 'deadly.' They may deny this and say that it's just sport, but points are given because if you really hit someone that hard you would do harm," Mr. Lee went on.

"Isn't that dangerous?" Henry blurted out. "What if they hit too hard and really hurt someone?"

"Good question. In full-contact sparring the fighters wear protective equipment on their hands and head like they do in boxing. The helmet and gloves are packed with some kind of plastic foam, but I can guarantee you that an inch or two of padding will not protect you from a full-contact punch or kick. The term 'full contact' means just that. A skillful punch or kick to a vital area like the head could be fatal; a punch or kick to the stomach or ribs, or back or joints could cripple a person for life. So what really happens, and everyone knows this is true, is that it's not really full contact but more like partial contact, which is still potentially lethal.

"Full contact also prevents good form. Contestants forget about proper form, because what's really on their minds is to score points and win a big trophy or a little fame. It's a way for someone who has been put down or pushed around to be a 'winner' in a short amount of time. They can feel good about themselves and for a brief moment forget about their real lives, where they may suffer from poverty or prejudice or whatever.

"I'm not blaming anyone and I'm not saying that what they're doing is bad and our way is good. It has nothing to do with good or bad. It's only that if the most important thing the martial arts can do is help us understand and resolve conflict peacefully, what is the most intelligent way to practice and improve our martial arts skills? If we look at it this way, we see that all this emphasis on tournament and sparring and self-defense has little value, because it's not helping to educate us about the true purpose of martial arts. It reduces martial arts to just a bunch of self-defense techniques, or just another sport. This is not wrong—the martial arts are great sports and certainly effective for self-defense—but that's not all they are. That's not why the martial arts were originally created. It is only a very narrow version, what they think the martial arts are, a way that promises to get one a lot of attention and self-satisfaction in a short time with very little real effort."

The contestants were starting to come out now. They were of all ages, from five or six up to older men and women, even some with white hair. Henry watched as nine square areas were set up in three rows around the large room. These square areas were called 'rings.' In each ring there were five officials, one sitting in each corner and one standing in the middle. There were both men and women officials.

Henry wasn't quite sure what was going on but as far as he could make out people who were going to spar signed in at a table and then put on their protective gear and went into the ring and bowed. Then they really started to go at it. He noticed that the form of most contestants was pretty sloppy compared to what he had seen at his school. It looked like they were interested in just knocking each other out. He didn't see much art in it at all.

In the rings the fighting continued to the cheers of the crowd. Henry noticed that many of the parents of the kids who were competing were down by the rings screaming at their kids to win. Parents of the losers would often get angry and yell at their kids. Some of the kids looked really upset if they didn't win, and some of the parents argued with the judges if they thought their children should have won. There seemed to be a lot of anger and frustration in the room.

"Can you see what I was talking about?" Mr. Lee broke into Henry's thoughts. "The difference between full contact and full power is that full-power techniques cannot make contact because it would be dangerous. But the main difference is that full-power freestyle is not meant as a contest or sport; it is not about winning or losing, as is full contact. Full power is a means to free yourself from fear, fear created by the way you think, like when we talked about what goes into a single punch. When you can move freely without self-conscious fear, which means thinking about how to protect yourself because you are afraid, then you have, at least for the moment, ended conflict in yourself. This may sound hard but it's actually quite simple. We do it in times of great danger when we forget ourselves to help others. The attention to the danger gives an urgency to the moment and then we act immediately. Like if you saw a small child run out into the street you would act immediately to save the child's life. You can feel that state of immediate action when you use full power in fixed or even more in freestyle."

"Do they have any real freestyle tournaments?" Henry asked.

"They used to, but rarely anymore. In the greatest one I ever saw there were two very skilled martial arts masters who met in a freestyle match. They bowed and faced each other, and their concentration was incredibly intense. But both were so skilled and their responsing ability so well developed that neither could detect any opening from the other. For the entire match nobody moved. It was truly amazing! They finally just bowed again to each other and left. The energy in that room was tremendous. Yet it seemed so natural, and even peaceful."

Later in the afternoon there were demonstrations of forms. Henry thought they were quite good but he was distracted by all the wild costumes and a circuslike atmosphere. Some students performed to rock music. It reminded Henry of the Ice Capades he had once seen, where everyone was dressed up in fancy costumes and skated to music. In fact, the forms demonstration looked like entertainment for the parents. One little girl about eight years old did a spectacular performance, appearing with a bunch of other kids, all in fancy uniforms and surrounded by flags, with patriotic music blasting. For a moment she was hidden by the others and then she suddenly reappeared in a baton twirler's outfit, throwing her baton high into the air and all to the beat of marching band music. Everyone was cheering like crazy. It reminded Henry of a half-time show at a football game.

Others performed with all kinds of dangerous weapons, with fierce looks on their faces and letting out wild screams at various points in the form. The fancier the outfit, it seemed to Henry, the wilder the performance; the louder the yells and the more intense the facial expressions, the crazier the crowd went and the bigger the trophy the contestant won. Some of the trophies were bigger than the kids who won them.

And yet in the midst of the circuslike atmosphere Henry noticed there were some great contestants, mostly kids he had seen at his own school, who demonstrated excellent forms wearing plain and simple martial arts uniforms, without any music or any Hollywood effects. Their performances were controlled and highly skilled. Even from his seat in the stands, Henry could see the beauty and the power of their forms. But few of them won trophies. It didn't seem fair, although Henry somehow sensed that they didn't really care.

"It looks like some people win just because they put on a better show," Henry remarked to Mr. Lee.

"That's very observant," replied Mr. Lee, "but you'll notice that those who concentrate on their forms have little time for all the silly showmanship. And probably don't care much about fancy trophies."

"But doesn't everyone really want to win?" asked Henry. "I mean, all athletes in all sports want to win because winning gets them money and fame, right?"

"I would say that's true for most," said Mr. Lee, "but there are still many who participate simply for the joy of the activity and to be the best at it they can. The true martial artist is looking for the self-understanding that will free him from fear and conflict. It may not seem so, but that's a greater accomplishment than becoming famous or wealthy."

"It sounds OK, but I still wouldn't mind being a famous sports star," said Henry. "All the reporters surround them at the games and everyone wants to meet them. It must be something to be like that. All the kids I know would give anything to meet a real star."

"Fame is a funny thing," said Ms. Watts, who had come to talk to Mr. Lee, and had overheard Henry. "We humans have a high opinion of ourselves. I saw a program on TV that compared the physical feats of humans with animals. The cheetah can run a lot faster than we can. The gorilla is much stronger; the monkey can climb higher and swing better; even a common squirrel can jump farther. But the one that really made me laugh, and showed how silly it is for humans to get so puffed up about their athletic skills, was a comparison between humans and ordinary fleas. The best human athletes can jump about seven feet high, whereas the flea can jump the equivalent of over a hundred feet."

Ms. Watts laughed and then said in a more serious tone, "I think that we need to put ourselves and our accomplishments into better perspective."

"I look at it from a different angle," said Mr. Lee. "I think to myself that there are over six billion people on earth. Each of us is like a tiny grain of sand on the Sahara Desert. Surely there are millions who are stronger, smarter, and better than we are, so why should we be so proud of ourselves? And the earth is only one of nine planets orbiting a sun that is only one of several billion stars in the Milky Way. The Milky Way is only one of thirty galaxies in a local cluster that is just a tiny speck in an ever-expanding universe.

"And we haven't even learned yet how to get to the next planet, so how can we possibly think we are so great? Envisioning all that I think should really make one humble. Do you know what humility means, Henry?"

"To not be mean or aggressive or something like that?" offered Henry.

"That's correct," said Mr. Lee, "but at the root of it all is simply not to take ourselves and our accomplishments so seriously. When we think that we or what we do are the most important thing there is, we have a tendency to put down others and their activities. We become arrogant, and even, as you say, aggressive. When we think too much of ourselves, our false pride can create great suffering. Pride in 'our' country, race, or religion can cause terrible conflict between us and others who are just as proud of 'their' country, race, or religion. The single most important goal of the martial arts that are for peace are that you understand this, and so be able to live humbly naturally. Not because someone tells you to be kind and humble, or rewards you if you are or punishes you if you aren't, but because you have seen the truth of your place in life. When you are content with yourself as only one grain of sand on the Sahara, or a tiny speck in an endless universe, you are truly humble."

Henry left that tournament that day with a new sense of what it is he was studying in martial arts. Even though he didn't understand everything completely, he did feel encouraged to study more, to practice more, because it felt right.

5 Intelligence

Understanding What Prevents Peace

"Do you know the story of the wise men and the elephant?" Sensei asked the class. It had been raining and now the sun was coming through the clouds, filling the room with light. An occasional cloud floated swiftly by, casting a temporary shadow. The birds started to sing as the air warmed.

"Once upon a time, there were four wise men who lived together in a small town," he began. "One day there was news of a great animal that was being brought to town. It was planned that the animal would appear as a grand surprise in the annual parade. The four wise men heard the news and very much wanted to see the animal before anyone else did. That way they could be the first to tell everyone what the animal was and everyone would believe that they were truly wise.

"They found out that the great animal was being hidden in a barn near the river. There was only one road to the barn and it was guarded so no one could see the great surprise until the parade the next day. The barn was heavily guarded too. The wise men decided to sneak through the thick woods around and behind the barn. If there were no guards, maybe they could get a peek at the animal through a window.

"Although the back of the barn was indeed unguarded, the wise men could see no windows or doors. But upon closer inspection they saw some knot holes in the wall, some

66

at eye level. Each wise man found a hole to look through, at four different places along the wall.

"'What do you see?' the first asked in a whisper.

"'I see a great snake! It's hanging from a wall and moving from side to side,' the second wise men exclaimed.

"'No, it's not a snake. It's a tiger with great long fangs!' the third wise man said excitedly.

"'What's wrong with you fools?' asked the fourth wise man. 'It's clearly a giant bird. I can see it flapping its great wings!'

"'No, you are all wrong. It is none of those. It's a giant fat pig, for I can see its huge belly,' the first one said.

"They argued and fought with each other all the way back to town. Each wise man was so sure of what he himself had seen that each told his friends and neighbors his own opinion about what the animal was. Each was sure that after the parade, he would be considered the wisest man of all.

"On the morning of the parade, the four wise men watched from a special viewing stand along with the mayor and other important people. Everyone had heard the different opinions of the wise men and all were anxious to know who was correct. All of a sudden a hush fell over the crowd and the great animal came into view, ambling down the street. It was plain as day what the animal was—an elephant! All the wise men were wrong!

"'Why, this isn't what any of you said it would be! How can all four of our town's wise men be wrong?' the mayor asked.

"The wise men stood there looking sheepish and embarrassed. Then they admitted how they had gone to sneak a look through the knotholes.

"A young boy listening to their confession laughed and said 'I know what happened. Because each of the wise men looked through a different hole, each saw a different part of the elephant. One saw the elephant's trunk and thought it was a big snake. Another saw the tusks and supposed it was a huge tiger. A third saw the elephant's big ears and concluded that they were the wings of a huge bird, while the last saw the huge belly and decided it was an enormous pig. And each was so sure that his view was right that he

didn't listen to the others to find out the truth.' It was obvious to the townspeople who the real wise man was that day."

The students had a good laugh at this story, and Sensei laughed with them.

"But there are some excellent lessons in the story of these foolish wise men," he said, "Can anyone guess what they are?"

"Maybe, don't be so quick to make a decision?" Henry asked.

"That's certainly one good lesson," Sensei agreed, "and what did the wise men base their decision on?"

A hand shot up from the back.

"Only a little part of the whole animal!" a little girl shouted.

"That's also correct," smiled Sensei. "Each of the wise men had his own opinion, his own prejudice, based on only a small part of the whole truth. Each made up his own mind and believed that his decision was correct."

"How is that prejudice?" Henry asked Sensei. "I mean, I thought that prejudice was hating people because their skin is a different color, or they come from another country."

"That's one kind of prejudice," replied Sensei. "Prejudice is made up of the words 'pre' and 'judge,' meaning to judge in advance, before all the facts are in. It is thinking or acting on the basis of wrong or incomplete information, like the wise men did. They all 'prejudged,' and because they did, they got into an argument over their opinions. This is a good example of how prejudice causes conflict.

"Remember that the basic goal of all martial arts is to understand and stop conflict. What this story has just told you is that conflict is created by people who think they know the truth and want to act on it. The fact is that in most cases what they believe is not the truth, as it is based on wrong or incomplete information.

"Let me give you another example. Suppose that at some time in your childhood you were bitten by a black-and-white dog. You remember it clearly; it was really painful. Now a few years later you're walking down the street and suddenly you see a black-and-white dog up ahead. How do you feel?" Sensei asked.

"I would feel afraid," said one of the younger students.

"Why?" Sensei responded.

"Because I would think that black-and-white dog is going to bite me. I think it's dangerous, so I feel afraid," the same student said.

"Exactly. You think that all black-and-white dogs are dangerous because you were bitten by one. But do you know that this dog is really dangerous? Is it the same dog that bit you before? What is the real truth? In fact, you are simply prejudiced. You're making a 'prejudgment.' You believe that all black-and-white dogs are dangerous because you were bitten by one. The brain has formed an image of that dog that bit you and, like movie film, has stored the images of 'fear, danger' together with 'black-and-white dogs' in your memory. Then whenever you see a black-and-white dog, you act on your pre-judgment, that stored information in your brain, and feel afraid." Sensei went on.

"Then, is that what happens when you look at someone with a different skin color or from a different part of the world from you?" Henry asked.

Sensei thought for a moment and then answered, "As I said, sometimes the information we have is incomplete, and sometimes it's just wrong. A black-and-white dog can bite. You know that; you have direct evidence. But do all black-and-white dogs bite? You don't know. Still, your experience has conditioned you to believe so. If you understand how your brain works, how it can remember something like a black-and-white dog biting you and then 'project' it onto a new dog, you will begin to understand how we are 'conditioned.' Suppose there's a part of town that's pretty poor and run-down. You hear someone say that people who live there are lazy or stupid and that's why they're poor. Your parents might say, don't go there at night because it's dangerous. You don't know anybody from that part of town, but you've heard all these things and they are filed in your brain. You have become conditioned. Are you following me?" asked Sensei.

Henry nodded with the rest of the class and said, "Yes, sir."

"Good," Sensei continued, "Now, suppose one day at school you meet a new student, let's say a friendly girl. You start talking with her and you ask where she's from. She says she's from that poor part of town. What will you think? What is going through your head? Be honest. Henry?"

"That maybe she's lazy, or not so smart, or at least maybe her parents are like that," replied Henry.

"Thank you for being honest," smiled Sensei. "Of course, you would think she wasn't very bright. You wouldn't be rude and call her stupid to her face, but if you were, say, choosing team members for a class project, you wouldn't choose her, would you? You would be prejudiced. You would be making a decision on the basis of wrong or incomplete information that you have been conditioned to believe.

"What I gave you, of course, is a very mild example. You only hurt her feelings. But conditioned thinking can make us go way beyond that, leading to violence and even to war. Conditioned thinking is the root of prejudice, and thus the cause of all conflict. It is why we can hate someone just because of their race or religion or skin color. The same conditioned thinking is at work, just like with the black-and-white dog. Either you have been scared or hurt by someone who is 'different' from you or someone has told you, probably over and over, that certain people are bad or dangerous or not to be trusted. The result is the same. The machine of prejudice, and the conflict it creates, is at work. Please spend some time thinking about this, because only when you truly understand it can you break the chains of conditioning.

"When I was young I watched a lot of Westerns on TV and in the movies. The so-called Indians were practically always bad—mean and untrustworthy—while the cowboys were the heroes. Those shows conditioned my thinking," Sensei went on explaining. "In the movies the cowboys killed the 'Indians' and didn't show any regret about it. When we played 'cowboys and Indians' as kids, no one wanted to be an Indian. We all wanted to be the cool cowboy hero, like John Wayne, who protected the white people from the dark 'savages.'

"Now we know that the term 'Indian' was just a mistake, a wrong identification—like that of the foolish wise men—made by white explorers who thought that they had reached the 'East Indies.' Today we use the term 'Native American' instead, because it shows respect for the fact that they were here in America long before our ancestors. When I finally met a real Native American for the first time, I was nervous. I felt a little guilty and at the same time a little afraid. I couldn't figure out why, but later realized that it was all that conditioning in my childhood. It's the same with all people we meet from other races, religions, and countries. We may not realize it but the movies in our brains are like the Western movies of my childhood, full of wrong or incomplete information. And when we meet someone who looks or acts different, the movies in our brain, right or wrong, begin to play.

"What we must try to do as martial artists is understand how conditioned thinking gives rise to prejudice and conflict, and so prevents peace. Just as we practice our physical self-defense skills, we must practice the mental martial arts, including working to become aware of our own conditioned thinking. We must carefully examine all those movies stored in our brains, discover how and where they are wrong or incomplete, and act accordingly. Our goal is to avoid prejudgments based on incomplete information, like the foolish wise men made; our goal is to see the *whole* truth with the common sense of the young boy. This is true intelligence, and part of the Code of Conduct for all martial artists that are for peace."

Kindness

Caring for Others as You Would Liked to Be Cared For

The hospital had a smell of strong soap. It was very clean and felt friendly. The doctors wore white coats but each had on a silly tie that made you feel good when you looked at it. The children's section was at the end of the hall. It was a large room with circus scenes painted on the walls. At the end of the room was a play area with lots of toys. Henry and the rest of the students, along with Ms. Watts, entered the room. They were dressed in their special martial arts outdoor "sports" uniforms. The only thing that distinguished them from regular jogging outfits was a small patch with their school logo on it.

The students of Henry's martial arts school had brought presents for the kids at the hospital. They also brought with them a puppet show they had put together with the help of Ms. Watts. This was a part of their community service time. In order to pass each test for rank advancement, all students had to spend a certain amount of time doing some helpful things in their community. Henry and some others had chosen to visit children at the local hospital.

After they had set up the puppet theater, one of the older students, who had changed into his regular martial arts uniform, stood in front of it and announced to the whole group, "Let me tell you the story of the Black Belt Warrior for Peace."

With the help of two nurses, all the sick children began to gather together. Some sat on the floor and some in chairs. Some had to sit in wheelchairs. There were some that were too sick and had to stay in their beds, but their beds were moved and turned so they could see. They all were curious about what would happen and paid great attention.

The older student standing in front of the theater began to tell the story:

"An evil old warrior and his band of powerful followers had been terrorizing the town where the Martial Arts for Peace School was." At this, the curtains parted and the evil warrior appeared. He was shouting at a young martial artist from the town.

"'We'll do whatever we want, and destroy anyone who gets in our way!' the old man threatened. 'And who is going to stop us?'

'No one,' said the young man as he softly smiled, which enraged the old warrior.

"'How are you going to defeat me, the greatest of all warriors? What are you going to do to escape from my power?' The old puppet warrior marched up and down in front of the young warrior.

"'Nothing,' said the young warrior for peace.

"'You're not going to fight me? You must be a coward. No doubt you have heard of my great powers that no one can get away from. My school of martial arts is the best there is. We have the best training and I have the strongest students. What school is yours?' the old warrior sneered.

"'We are from the school of No Sword, the Martial Arts for Peace School. We do not fight when we do not have to. Our way is to subdue the enemy without fighting,' the young warrior for peace replied calmly.

"'Then we will defeat you. You are weak and we are strong. You cannot defeat us so we will take over your school,' the old warrior went on boastfully.

"'No, that will not happen. You cannot defeat us because we have the most powerful weapon. This weapon will not hurt you but you cannot win over it,' the young warrior replied with a calm and confident voice.

"'Nothing can defeat us. We are bigger and stronger than you, so how can you possibly imagine you can defeat us? What weapon is so great that it can beat us?' the old warrior responded with a very small note of uncertainty in his voice.

"'We have been trained not only in physical martial arts but also in Mental Martial

76

Arts, which is mightier than all the weapons you have. Our greatest Martial Arts for Peace weapon is truth and beauty. Give up now and we will be kind to you.'

"'Never will we give up,' roared the old warrior with anger. 'You are an arrogant young man, and your words offend me. You have until dawn to surrender or we will attack.'

"The next morning, as the old warrior and his band headed toward the town to attack the Martial Arts for Peace School, they saw the young man standing in a field. But before the old warrior could even draw his sword, the young warrior started to sing the most beautiful song the old man had ever heard. The pure words of the song told of love and kindness. It told of a kingdom of peace in a lush and beautiful valley where all people lived with kindness and caring. The song rose up to the heavens and spread out into the hills and the mountains beyond. The song was so beautiful that it softened the old warrior's heart and raised his spirits until he began to cry from happiness.

"'Oh, how beautifully you sing,' cried the old warrior, his eyes full of tears of joy. 'Never in all these years have I ever heard such beauty and truth. The world seems so wonderful now that I can see the good in it. Your song has given me a feeling of joy that I cannot describe in words. My heart was cold and I couldn't feel anything. Your song opened my heart so I can feel again. You've given me new life. You truly are a warrior for peace and I surrender to your power. All I ask is to become your student and learn from you to be so powerful that you can defeat the enemy without fighting.'"

The little kids liked the story and clapped when it was finished. Henry and the other puppeteers performed a few other short plays about bullying and resolving conflict peacefully. They used the puppets to show how they could escape potential conflict by using their brains instead of their fists. This was exactly what Henry and the other students had been learning at their martial arts school. It was really fun to use the puppets to act out the same situations. It also helped Henry to understand better the lessons he was being taught by his teachers, and he even thought of some new ideas about how to defeat the bully without fighting.

After the puppet shows the martial arts students played a few games with the children. One was called "Sensei Says," and was like the old game "Simon Says." In this game the children had to imitate moves that the student in front did. If he said, "Sensei says,

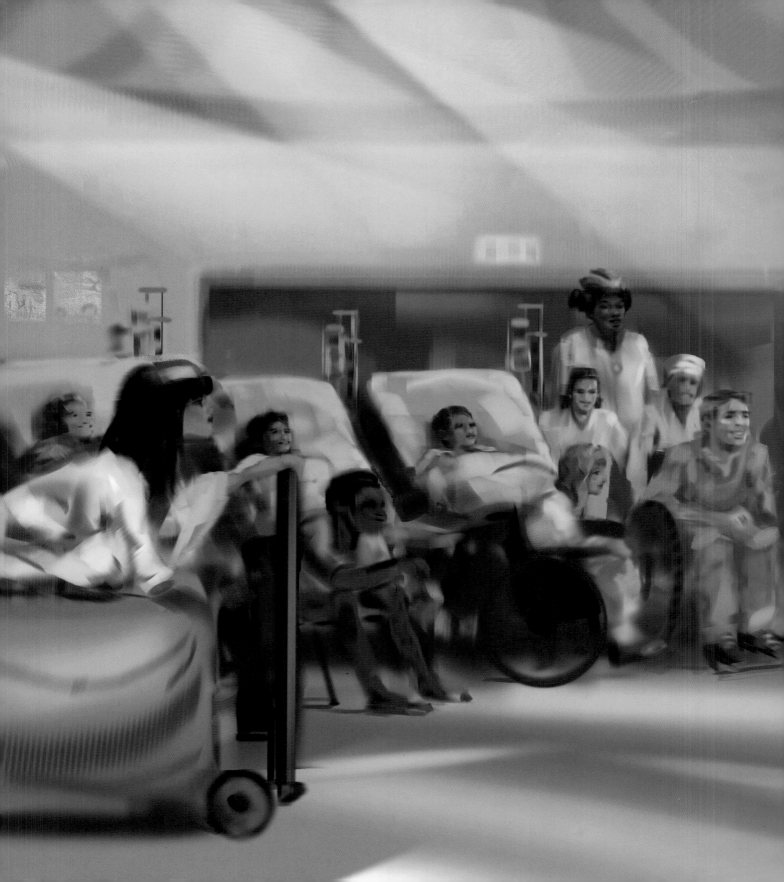

move your right hand," they would have to move their right hand. But if the student in front just said, "Move your right hand," without saying "Sensei Says" first, the person was out of the game. The students made it really easy so no one felt bad about losing. They all had a good laugh. It was then that Henry realized the value of laughter and how it could make a person feel much better.

After their planned program, the martial arts students got a chance to talk to the children and to answer questions about their training.

"Can you break bricks?" one kid about six asked shyly.

"Only if I'm attacked by bricks," a senior student said with a smile.

"Can you leap tall buildings and disappear into the night?" another kid asked. "I've heard Ninjas can do that."

"Ninjas like that are in the movies. The real Ninjas were trained killers who weren't so peaceful. You wouldn't want to meet one. We are Martial Artists for Peace. Some of you may think that sounds strange, but it's true. We try to stop fights using mental self-defense rather than physical self-defense. We learn many ways to talk the bully out of hurting us. Don't get me wrong; we still practice physical self-defense skills, but that's because knowing how to protect ourselves gives us the confidence not to fight.

"Real martial arts are fun, but it's not what you see in the movies or on TV. That's not real martial arts. It's just pretend fighting. In fact, I don't think it's good for children to watch that stuff. I used to watch it and I got nightmares."

As Henry listened he realized that many of the questions the kids were asking were the same ones he had when he first started training at his martial arts school. And they had the same wrong impressions about the martial arts that he did before. It was interesting to see how so many people could have the same wrong ideas. He realized that he too had been conditioned, programmed like a computer, to think that the martial arts were just cool secret techniques used to beat up bad guys. And then he thought, instead of watching bad guys and good guys in action films, wouldn't it be better if everyone did their part to fight crime and poverty in real life? If everyone really wanted to right the world's wrongs, to stop the bad guys, why didn't they become real rangers and police officers instead of watching made-up stories on TV? Henry had come to have little respect for the "heroes" of the big screen. He now had more respect for the ordinary heroes of real life—policemen, firemen, teachers, social workers—who tackled the poverty, prejudice, injustice, and dangers of the real world every single day. In fact, it was really unfair that those movie stars should get so much money for *pretending* to do what those underpaid heroes of real life actually *did* do.

They all talked about illness too. Some of the kids were really sick, which really made Henry sad.

"Why did you come here?" one little kid in bed asked weakly looking directly at Henry.

Henry couldn't think of any answer except to say, "Because we love you." It just came right out of his mouth without thinking. He had never used the word "love" before, except to his parents. He was surprised both at the question and his answer, but was even more surprised at the next question from the same boy.

"Why do you care?" he said.

There was silence in the room for what seemed like a long time. Henry then said something that he didn't really understand. He could really feel it though.

"Because we're all in this together. Life, that is. I mean, that we all have the same problems and we all want to be cared for and helped. We want to care for others because it feels good to be cared for."

The little boy in the big hospital bed just smiled. That was his reply. Henry never forgot that day and the many days he spent visiting the hospital. He learned a valuable lesson: that the most powerful weapon in the world is something that we all have and can use whenever we want. It won't hurt anyone, and yet it can win over almost everyone and can never be defeated. That weapon is kindness.

7 Order

After forms practice, Ms. Watts invited the students to sit on the floor around her. "Let me tell you some stories about famous martial artists," she said. "I won't mention names because I don't think that matters. Some people might think that names are very important, but I would rather let the story be the lesson than the person. People today seem overly fascinated with celebrity; everyone seems to be looking for heroes to worship. This is not a healthy attitude. Remember that the essence of all martial arts is the 'empty self.' This means being empty of self-importance, empty of the need, as the expression goes, 'to *be* somebody.' It means accepting who we really are, nobody important. It may sound strange, but there is great joy in being nobody. When you accept yourself as nobody, when you have forgotten the 'you,' there comes a wonderful freedom from all anxieties, which really are just concerns about the self. I know many of you have probably had that feeling—maybe when you see a beautiful sunset, or smell a fragrant flower, or see the night sky with a billion stars twinkling above—of being at one with the world, totally lost in it. In that moment 'you' are not there, 'you' are 'empty.' At that moment there is total order. Life is in harmony with itself because 'I' am not interfering, 'I' am not important. Disorder comes from trying to be someone, trying to become important or powerful. Real order, in which there is no

82

conflict, is peace. We cannot bring about order or peace; it comes only when we understand the disorder in ourselves.

"The stories I'm going to tell you are about order and disorder. The first story is about a martial arts teacher who creates order by not trying to be important. One day this teacher took his martial arts students on an outing up into the hills above their town. They were with their chief instructor, who felt it was important to get out into nature. 'You've seen the waves of the ocean,' he said in the quiet of the night, 'now listen to the waves of the pines.' The wind had picked up and was blowing through the tops of the tall pine trees on the hill. Listening carefully, the students heard the rustling of the top branches and they forgot themselves for that moment. There was just the wind and the pine trees.

"They sat down on some rocks and the still-warm bare ground and began to recite poetry. 'It is important for you to be educated martial artists,' the chief instructor said, 'We've studied music, architecture, herbs, and many other arts. Now let us try to appreciate poetry and literature.'

"After about two hours of reading poetry and discussing various books they had read, the chief instructor called for an end to the gathering and they started down the hill toward town. On the way they heard some men yelling below them on the trail. The chief instructor sent one of his students ahead to see what was going on. The student crept carefully down the trail and came upon a group of drunken men who worked in the mines near town. Apparently they had been celebrating because they were shouting and fighting among themselves. The student, unseen by the men, went back up to where the others were waiting. After explaining what was going on below the chief instructor turned his group back up the hill and down the other side and took the long way home," Ms. Watts concluded her story.

The students were silent and looked a bit confused. "Why did they do that?" one of the younger students asked. "They could have easily defended themselves if the drunken men caused trouble. They knew the martial arts."

"That's what we're trying to help you understand. Our martial arts teach ways to avoid and therefore prevent conflict. The chief instructor knew that his students might be challenged to a fight by that group of tough miners, so he avoided a potential conflict by going around it even if it took longer," Ms. Watts responded.

"But they would be called 'chicken' today if they didn't fight," another student spoke out.

"By 'chicken' I presume you mean coward. That's unfortunately true, isn't it? That's what we see in action films where the 'hero' or 'good guy' fights with the 'bad guy' because he can't lose face, he can't back down. A real hero is one who avoids a fight, not starts one. But I guess that just isn't exciting. A person of peace is not honored but a violent persons is. The world is truly upside down. I think that you all know the truth: Being peaceful takes a great deal of strength and courage. Hurting someone doesn't.

"Here's another true story. It's about one of the students of that same group of martial artists as the last story. This happened just after World War II in a country that had suffered terribly from the fighting. This student was walking along a back-country road when he was attacked by a desperate and frightened man. With no time to use his mental martial arts, and knowing how to defend himself physically, he grabbed his attacker in a hold that prevented him from moving. He held the man until some people nearby called the police and took him away. The martial arts student never told anyone about what happened until long afterward, when he was in his eighties. And when he finally told it, he felt ashamed that he had to use physical force on a poor and desperate man who was probably just hungry and had nothing to eat. The martial arts student felt sorry for the man and wished that he had had the time to avoid or resolve the conflict before it got to the physical level. He also confessed that the incident was the first and only time that he had ever used the physical martial arts on anyone.

"Can all of you see that this student of the martial arts had the right attitude? Although he trained almost his whole life in the martial arts, he was truly a man of peace. To many people this may sound strange, but it's true. If a person just studies a martial art to gain fame, or to win at tournaments, or to make money then this cannot lead to understanding and peace. But if a person studies the martial arts to learn about conflict and how to prevent it, then that person can be a peacemaker. But one has to study the whole of the martial arts, not just a part. One cannot study the physical part alone without the larger picture of the mental.

"Here is another story for you to think about. This one concerns martial arts teachers who create disorder by trying to be more powerful, more important. It may be a bit more difficult at first to understand. There was a certain student of martial arts who went to a country in the Far East to study with some of the greatest living masters. One lived far away from any town, high in the mountains, where he trained every day in the forest. The student was given permission by this famous teacher to study with him. As they practiced their forms together every day, the student noticed that this teacher had large and tough-looking hands that were callused and hardened, especially the first two knuckles on each hand. The student was curious about why his teacher's hands were like this and was soon to find out the reason.

"One day the teacher took the student out into the forest and stopped by a grove of trees. One of the large trees had part of its surface worn bare. It had a slight indentation in it where the wood had been discolored and was darker than the rest. The teacher stopped in front of the tree and positioned himself in a martial arts stance and began to punch the tree with his bare hands. He kept on punching the tree for a long time, becoming more and more intense. He finally stopped after giving a tremendous yell. He then motioned the student to do the same.

"The student positioned himself in front of the tree and began to hit it with his fists. At first it hurt his hands, but after a minute or two his hands became numb and he no longer felt the pain. He did it for a while longer until he noticed that the wood of the tree looked dark red. He then realized that his knuckles were bleeding and he stopped. They looked terrible. The pain came back as the numbness wore off. He then looked at the tree and felt a deep sadness that he allowed himself to hit such a beautiful tree.

"The next day the student was wakened early by the teacher. The student's hands ached terribly. Blood had soaked through the bandage he had put over his bloody knuckles. The teacher led him down the mountain to a farm below. There he saw a large fenced-in area with some bulls wandering peacefully around. A man who apparently owned the farm greeted the teacher with a deep and respectful bow. They were led to a part of the fenced-in area in which there was a lone, smaller bull. The bull looked nervous to the student. It kept circling the smaller pen trying to find a place to get out. The student could feel the bull's fear. The teacher stepped into the small pen and approached the bull. The bull stopped moving and faced the tough-looking martial arts teacher. The student watched with terror as he saw the bull back away in the pen and then, when there was no more room for the bull to go, it charged the man. The martial arts teacher quickly stepped aside and as the bull passed him he struck the bull on top of it's head with his large hardened hand, stunning the bull. The bull turned with a dazed look and tried to charge the man again but this time the man grabbed the bull by the horns and began to pound away at the bull's head until the bull was bloody. The bull let out terrible screams, his eyes rolling wildly as he fell to the ground under the beating of this man. The teacher kept on beating the bull in the head until the bull's body began to twitch and finally stopped dead. The teacher grabbed the bloody head of the bull and pounded on one of its horns until it ripped off, leaving a great mass of bloody skin hanging from where the horn used to be. The teacher, with blood all over his martial arts uniform, stood up triumphantly, with the mangled horn in his hand and let out a terrifying scream of victory. The student went behind the barn and got sick there. He sat for awhile in the dirt and cried like he had never cried before. Before the teacher could find him he ran away into the woods."

"Why did the teacher kill the bull?" one of the students asked with pain in her voice.

"Is that a true story?" another student asked with disbelief.

"Yes, it is true," Ms. Watts replied. "It is based on the life of a 'famous' martial arts master. He killed many bulls with his bare hands just to prove how strong he was. I am ashamed to even call him a 'martial artist,' and I certainly would never call him a teacher. I find it unbelievable that people studied with this person and that they called him a 'master.'"

"What happened to the student?" Henry asked.

"I'm glad you asked," smiled Ms. Watts, "because there's more to the story. The student believed deep in his heart that somewhere he would find a true teacher, so he left the mountains and continued his search. He came to a small village where there was a martial arts master famous for teaching a 'spiritual' martial art. The student asked for directions to the master, who lived alone in the foothills just beyond town. The student approached the master's cottage and asked to be taught by him. The master didn't say anything, but motioned the student to follow him up a path to a grove where there was a high waterfall splashing into a pool below. The teacher took off the top of his martial arts outfit and went into the pool, where he sat upon a rock directly under the rushing

water. The student followed, entering the pool and sitting next to the teacher under the freezing water. They both sat there for a long while. The student was freezing and began to shiver uncontrollably. He wanted to get out and started to, when the teacher stopped him. The student tried to sit longer but even though he was somewhat numb he couldn't stop shivering. He knew that he would get sick if he stayed there any longer. He finally got up quickly before the teacher could prevent him and took the top of this uniform and his backpack and left the older man sitting under the waterfall.

"Back in town, the student asked about this teacher. The townspeople told him that this martial arts master vowed that he would sit under the waterfall and never speak to anyone until he became enlightened. All that night the student thought about his experiences with the two 'masters.' The next morning he left the Far East and returned home.

"What was this martial arts teacher trying to get? What is 'enlightenment?'" a student asked.

"As you study the martial arts you will sooner or later come across this interesting word. 'Enlightenment' has been given many meanings by many people, including some people who just love to confuse simple things with fancy-sounding words. For now, let's just think of 'enlightenment' as being truly aware, as experiencing life without the interference of our thoughts, our fears, and regrets.

"Think of being enlightened as the way we were when we were small children. Everything was new to us, and we lived from moment to moment, aware of life, aware of what was happening, but not thinking about it. We could forget what happened to us quickly. We didn't remember what hurt us yesterday or worry about what was going to happen tomorrow. We didn't have much of a past to remember, and the future was completely unknown to us. We simply lived in what might be called the 'here and now.' And life was for the most part wonderful, and full of endless surprises. This order, this peace, was natural, not imposed through self-centered thinking. But then we all started to grow up. We started to think too much, to regret our past mistakes and to worry about what the future held. We lost our 'innocence,' which is a good word for our early childhood years. Remember, if I use a word you don't know, please look it up in the dictionary.

"As we grew up, we became trapped by our thoughts and the feelings that go with them. We became less aware of the natural order of the world around us—the trees, plants, and sky that had given us so much happiness as children. We sort of fell slowly asleep and were not even aware of it.

"Then one day, when we became sick with too much conflict created by fretting about every little thing, we suddenly wanted to be free like innocent little children again. So we started doing childish things. But that's a mistake; what we really should be seeking is to be 'childlike,' not childish. But to do that we need to realize our dilemma and do the real work of trying to understand what created the disorder in the first place. The real work is discovering how our thinking—our regrets about the past and our fears about the future—has created a 'prison' in our heads in which we feel trapped. We need to see the disorder that this creates, in our lives and in the world.

"Can we return to watching the world in awe and wonder as we did as children? We need to see the world as it is, as it is really happening, without trying always to change it. By watching in that way we can be free. We become aware that most of our thinking is wasteful or destructive, and that we don't need to think in those old ways. When we see the disorder that such thinking has created, we begin to discover order. When we discard the useless and wasteful thoughts, we see that the thoughts left over are practical and necessary. This is real enlightenment.

"Unfortunately the real meaning of enlightenment has been misunderstood. People have done many childish things trying to regain that wonderful innocent feeling of youth. They sit silently under freezing waterfalls, they repeat slogans over and over, they even pay therapists to tell them not to worry so much.

"Students, there are many traps and temptations in life that will lead you to dead ends. There are many false teachers who will want you to make them into your heroes. How are you going to find out what is true or not? You are young now and may not grasp everything we are saying, but you soon will. We need to start to introduce these insights to you now so you can begin to develop an understanding that will help keep you out of trouble later on. Just hold on, work hard, and trust your own eyes and ears.

8 Responsibility

Meeting Life's Challenges with a Brave Spirit

The class were all dressed in their special martial arts sports outfits to visit a home for the elderly. Henry had never been to one and was a bit uncomfortable. He expected to see a lot of old people who were sick and dying, and he wasn't sure how he should act or what he should say. He had felt this way before visiting the children's ward also, but the patients there were all kids, who he could talk to. Unfortunately, two of the kids he had met there had died recently, but he still remembered the fun of being with them. They laughed at their visitors' jokes and wanted the students to do the puppet plays over and over. It was as if they had forgotten that the plays had already been performed many times and everything was brand-new. It amazed Henry to see this. It also surprised him to see how well they accepted their condition.

The building they were led into looked friendly from the outside. It was surrounded by a pretty woods with a pond in back. Ducks floated lazily in the pond and the air smelled of spring flowers. Inside the building the students were led down a corridor whose walls were covered with beautiful paintings. At the end of the corridor they went into a large colorful room that also smelled of flowers. Some people were sitting in ordinary chairs and others were in wheelchairs. Henry was surprised at what he saw. He expected these old people to be just old. He remembered his grandfather and how old he looked. He also remembered that old smell of his grandfather that had made Henry feel a bit nauseous. But here in this room he felt none of that.

They had gone to the center, which the residents referred to as the Elder Center, to teach some of the yoga stretching exercises they had learned at their martial arts school. When Henry first did the exercises himself he felt great. They relieved his tension and made him feel more peaceful. After the yoga session the students sat down to talk with the residents. Before the visit Mr. Lee had talked with them about the importance of elderly people and how in other times and cultures they had been far more greatly respected for their wisdom. Native Americans, as well as other tribal groups around the world, gave their elders a special place in their society so that they could learn from their many years of experience. In recent times, however, seniors were more often pushed aside for the young, but Mr. Lee advised the students to ask questions and listen carefully, for the seniors were still a great source of knowledge from which the young could learn.

"You young people have a lot of energy," a woman spoke kindly after the yoga session ended. "I'm Maude. It's wonderful to watch your grace and strength."

Henry smiled at the compliment, but didn't know what to say, except, "Thank you, ma'am. I'm Henry."

"And that's good, because you'll need it to meet the many challenges you will face in life," another senior chimed in. "Remember, life is a serious game, to be played as best as you can. The goal is to play it with the fewest errors possible."

"Yes, Frank," said the kindly woman, "but we can't be too hard on ourselves. If a baseball player hits only one-third of the time he's considered a great batter. That's only about three hits out of ten." She turned to Henry, "So don't be too hard on yourself. When you fall down, and you will, just get back up as soon as possible and go on."

"But learn from your mistakes, so that next time you won't fall so hard on your keester," Frank laughed. "Any other questions about the meaning of life?"

Before he began taking martial arts classes, Henry never had long or serious conversations with any adults except for his parents. His parents tried hard to help him understand what he was going through as he grew up, and Henry got along with them well. But since beginning his study of martial arts, he had more opportunity to talk with

adults, not only with Sensei, Ms. Watts, and Mr. Lee but with other people who visited the class to share their knowledge. Other adults had come to talk to the students about art, music, poetry, and even subjects like world affairs. Sensei had told them many times that he felt it was important to be an "articulate" martial artist. Henry didn't know what that meant and so, as he had been told to do, he looked it up in a dictionary. It meant "to speak clearly and well."

Sensei had explained to the students, "The martial arts student needs to be able to speak clearly and well about the 'art' of the martial arts. The student needs to be educated, needs to be able to tell others the real significance and value of martial arts that are for peace and how it can help people to understand and resolve conflict peacefully."

Sensei told the class that by visiting seniors you could learn a great deal, but that you had to ask intelligent questions and, most importantly, you really needed to listen. Listening meant that you had to put aside all your opinions and start afresh. But it didn't mean to accept without question what someone else said; you had to find out for yourself what was true but you had to really listen to find out anything new and valuable.

"I do have a question," Henry heard himself saying. "What's it like getting old? I can't imagine it."

"At your age it is not something you need to be too concerned with and that's fine," said a man in a wheelchair. "But it may help you begin to understand what life will hold for you later on. And this is very hard to know because although all of us are essentially the same, each one of us is uniquely different. Some of us are born with strong genes that we've inherited from our ancestors. And some of us are born weak and have to struggle most of our lives. Life is not fair, and that's one of life's tough lessons."

"But I can assure you that the quality of life will be better if you take care of yourself," one of the oldest and healthiest looking elders spoke knowingly. His name tag identified him as Fred.

"We've been learning about things like healthy eating and exercise. What else can we do to stay healthy?" one of Henry's fellow students asked.

"I've been a vegetarian for over fifty years and I know how well I feel because of it," replied Fred. "I never wanted to kill animals and eat them. I had pets all my life and so I loved animals. It's hard for me to understand how people can say that they love their dogs and cats but eat other equally wonderful animals. It's a terrible thing to kill them when we don't really need to. I think that most people are used to it and are afraid to stop because they think they will get sick if they do. The opposite is actually true. You will get much more healthy not eating meat. I believe now that not eating meat can prevent many types of cancer.

"But there is also something very important you must do to keep yourself healthy. It has to do with the way you think and therefore the way you feel. The way you think and feel creates what you believe and what you believe, your attitude about life, determines how you live. If you let your mind dwell on anxieties about what you've done or must do, or what someone has done to you or might do to you, you'll begin to live with fear and hate, and that's not healthy. So begin to understand what thinking is and what some types of thoughts can do to create conflict in your life and the lives of others."

The mention of fear was very interesting to Henry. He thought to himself that these seniors didn't have to worry about what others thought of them. Their lives were nearly over. They certainly didn't have to worry about bullies.

"Then, are you afraid of death?" Henry asked, not sure it was a proper question.

"What a good question!" Maude said happily. "Death is part of life. In fact, think about it: one can't be without the other. There would be no such thing as death if there weren't life. So everything that lives must die. But is that something to fear?

"I wouldn't be telling the truth if I said I never give it a thought. But then I remember how when I was a child I used to watch carefully how the autumn leaves turned colors and fell from the trees. They just seemed to 'die.' It made me sad. But late in the winter I would look closely at the tree's branches where the leaves had fallen. Along the twigs where the leaves used to be were tiny new buds, which would blossom when the weather turned warmer into new light-green leaves. It made me feel such joy! And I always wondered: could I ever feel such joy if the leaves had simply been endlessly green forever? What gave me joy was witnessing the endless cycle of birth, death, and rebirth."

Another senior in a wheelchair, Barbara, spoke up, "That reminds me of when I first saw a redwood tree in California. You know redwoods can grow to be huge, with trunks so big some have been carved out so you can drive your car through. But have you ever seen a redwood tree seed? It's really tiny. I was amazed when I held one of those tiny, tiny seeds in the palm of my hand and looked up at that wonderful giant of a tree. It seemed impossible that such an enormous tree could grow out of such a small seed. But what amazed me even more was thinking that this tiny seed in my hand held the infinite possibility of redwood trees. What I mean is, that tiny seed could grow a redwood tree that would have a seed that would grow another redwood tree and so on, endless trees, from seed to tree to seed to tree. And all living things, including humans, are like this. I remember a poem about it; would you like to hear it?"

"Yes, please," said several students.

"It goes something like this:

> *The morning glory blooms but for an hour*
> *and yet it differs not at heart*
> *from the giant Redwood*
> *that lives for a thousand years"*

"Are you saying that we're like the trees, that each one of us came from a seed and will grow like a tree and then become a seed again and so on?" asked a red-haired girl.

"Yes, in a manner of speaking," said Barbara. "But this doesn't mean having children and then they have children. Remember there are many leaves and many branches of the tree. And many seeds fall. The individual may die, but the group carries on, whether redwoods or humans."

"Um, with all due respect, how do you know that's true?" the red-haired girl replied. "Sorry, but at our martial arts school we're taught to question everything we don't understand. Is this just your opinion?"

"Nature doesn't lie," Barbara replied. "The truth is there right in front of us all the time. It is not a belief or an opinion. The problem comes from the fact that most people don't see themselves as a part of nature. They see nature as something separate from themselves. But it wasn't always like this. In ancient times we lived closer to nature, and felt a part of it. But today we live in heated or air-conditioned buildings and rarely go out into nature for any amount of time, so we've become cut off from its lessons about life and death."

"But where do we go when we die?" the girl persisted.

"Where does the leaf go?" Barbara replied thoughtfully. "I suppose none of us really knows."

"I think that I'm curious about death because it scares me sometimes," the girl said softly. "My grandmother died last year. She died at home and a group of people from 'Home Hospice' came to our house and took care of her and made her feel more comfortable. I remember her funeral when I got to see her in the casket. She looked so peaceful lying there. I thought that she might open her eyes and get up and walk away. The service was so pretty and I had a wonderful feeling that death was something beautiful and not at all frightening. But then I thought of her body lying in the dark and cold, never being able to speak with anyone again. It seemed so lonely. Then I started to have nightmares about death."

"I guess since none of us has experienced it, we can't truly say what it is," Harold said. "But let's play a little game. This could be interesting."

He got up and wrote on a pad in big letters the words, "Death is _____." "Now I want you to tell me the first thing that comes into your mind when you read this," he said. " Don't think, just finish the sentence and I'll write down your answers."

The responses came quickly.

"Death is the ending of everything."

"Death is becoming dust again, like we once were."

"Death is a dark black hole."

"Death is going to heaven to be with God."

"Death is disappearing into space."

"Death is seeing my grandmother again."

"Death is the unknown."

"Now, answer this next question," said Harold. "How do you know what you just said to be true?"

The students thought about it for a minute and then one answered, "Because that's what I was told death was."

"So you were told that death was a black hole or the end of everything or the unknown. Now is that death or is it just some people's opinion of what death must be? What are the real facts about death? What do we really know?"

"I guess what scares me is what I've been told about death. I thought about it and I had bad dreams," the red-haired student answered.

"Sure, we can be scared by what other people tell us about death. But the experience of death itself is unknown. Why should we be afraid of what we don't know? What we are afraid of is only what we think death is."

"But we can see someone dying, like my grandmother."

"Dying is different than death. If you think about it, we all start to die the minute we're born. We all grow older and get closer to death. So we can experience dying because we can watch it in ourselves and others, and in nature, like when we see leaves dying. This is just a fact of life."

"And hopefully, if we have led an intelligent life, we will die with dignity," another senior spoke for the first time. "So it is important to live a good life. We should focus on living well. That will take care of dying well."

"Another important thing to ask is, 'Who dies?'" Frank said. "I know that sounds strange, but I mean who is it really that is afraid to die? We can see that the body gets old and stops working properly. But which part of you is afraid of death? I've read something about the philosophy of the martial arts, and I think that you'll find that the answer to that question has something to do with the 'empty self' that you've probably heard of. As a matter of fact, I read an interesting martial arts story that may help you make some sense of life and death. Would you like to hear it?"

"Yes, please," several students spoke in unison.

"One hot autumn day, a student was sitting on a riverbank with his teacher." Frank began. "They had been practicing their forms in the hot sun and were trying to cool off. The student gazed around him and noticed that the leaves were turning red and brown, some falling from the trees. Winter would be coming soon.

"'It's so beautiful,' the student turned to his teacher and remarked, 'but isn't it sad that all these beautiful things in nature will die soon? Where do they come from and where do they go?'

"The teacher smiled and said, 'It's too hot a day for such hard questions! But fetch me a glass of ice water, and maybe we can think about it together.'

"The student brought the glass of ice water to his teacher and sat beside him again. The teacher took a sip, then placed the glass in front of him and looked at it with appreciation.

"'Absolutely delicious! Ice is a wonderful thing, isn't it?' he asked.

"'I suppose so,' said the student, not giving the comment much thought.

"'What is ice, anyway?' asked the teacher.

"'Why, just frozen water,' answered the student, surprised. He hoped that the teacher would begin to speak about death, but the old man just lapsed into silence and stared intently at the glass. The student knew not to interrupt him at such moments, but waited patiently for him to speak.

"After a long while the teacher asked, 'What happened to the ice?'

"'Gone, melted,' said the student.

"'Then, there's your answer,' the old man said.

"'I'm not sure I understand,' the student replied, although he was beginning to realize what his teacher was talking about.

"'If I told you, 'What once was is now again; what is now will be again,' you might think I was just being confusing or trying to sound profound,' the teacher said, 'but I don't have to say anything. It's all evident in a glass of ice water or the world around us. From water to ice to water is a natural transformation that anyone can understand; the changing seasons is something we can all observe. If we can delight in the cycle of the seasons, why not in the cycle of humanity?'

"The teacher took the glass of water and poured it slowly into the river. 'What comes from the source of life returns to it. The river flows and on it goes, from nothing to nowhere. Why should we be any different?'

"The student bowed and left this teacher sitting by the river."

The afternoon was coming to a close when Henry and the martial arts students left the Elder Center. They had talked of many things that day, of hardships and joys, of family and friends. But what had interested Henry the most were their insights about death, and how in the end we are all equal. He felt strange comfort knowing that he was not alone. Like leaves on a tree, autumn comes for us all, but the tree of life goes on producing new green buds each spring, year after year after year. Henry left with a new respect for how much these elders had to teach younger people. The students thought of them as Warriors for Peace, who have faced the challenges of life with a brave spirit and persevered.

Wisdom

Living Without Fear

9

Henry learned about the wisdom of the Mirror of Truth the day he passed his first belt-rank test. It was a lesson he was never to forget. It started with the test itself. He and eight others were going up for the same rank. The senior students were to be tested later that same day. The test started out with everyone sitting quietly for about ten minutes, which seemed like an hour. Every class they sat silently for a few minutes but never this long. Henry's thoughts were all over the place. His teachers called it the "monkey mind," where your thoughts jump all over like monkeys in the trees.

He was worried about passing the test. He had practiced very hard on both the mental and physical parts but wasn't sure he knew them well enough. He had very high standards for himself and he worried that what he knew didn't live up to his best. He didn't want to fail and be left behind. He had seen some students not pass the test and have to stay at the same level until the next time. His teachers had spoken to the class about this. They said that it was important to learn from failure, that failure is just a temporary state because if you learned from it you would move on and advance even further in your understanding of the martial arts and life.

Henry and the eight other students went through their forms and seemed to do well. None of the teachers said anything to them. Henry couldn't tell from their faces if they approved or disapproved. Then came the mental test. Henry had read all the books that were assigned for this level and did his book reports on them. He had private discussions with Mr. Lee and Ms. Watts about parts he was having trouble with. He didn't understand everything he read. Some of it made sense and he could see how understanding what was said in the books helped him in his daily life, as his teachers said it would. They had told all of them over and over that it took time to fully understand what they were saying to them and what was written in the books. They reminded them all that they had to work at it. Still, no matter how hard he had tried, he felt very unsure of what he knew.

They all sat down in a circle with their teachers, and Sensei joined them for this part.

"I wonder if you really know who you are." Sensei said to the nervous group. "Who you think you are or who you think you should be are very different from who you actually are. In order to be free of conflict, which is the basic intent of all martial arts that are for peace, you will have to look into the Mirror of Truth."

Henry didn't quite understand what his teacher was saying but it made him even more nervous on hearing it. He had never heard of the Mirror of Truth before. As Henry was thinking about it Sensei must have read his thoughts because at that very moment he pulled out a common hand mirror and held it up to Henry's face. For a moment Henry didn't recognize who he was looking at in the mirror. He saw a face that looked like all faces, a human face with no name. But then in a flash he saw himself! He saw a worried face as if all his thoughts and emotions were reflected on it for all to see. He also felt a sudden unpleasant feeling in his stomach and chest. He now saw his face and didn't like what he saw. He didn't want to look and quickly let his gaze fall to the ground.

Sensei moved the mirror along in front of all the faces of the students, pausing for a moment with each person. He then turned the mirror over and looked into it himself and laughed.

"So who are you? Or who do you think you are? Did you see yourself in the Mirror of Truth? As you can see, this mirror isn't magical. It is just a common mirror anyone can buy at the store. But it's amazing in that it tells the truth. A mirror simply reflects what's there. It doesn't lie. But we do. We lie about ourselves and the mirror shows us the truth. We lie about who we are and who we think we should be. Perhaps 'lie' is too strong a word. Maybe I should say the mirror reveals our false perceptions about ourselves. What did you see? Does anyone want to share what they saw?"

"I saw for a moment someone beautiful and then what I saw became very painful," said one of the very pretty girls there. "I didn't like who I was. I looked too fat and ugly," she said with pain in her voice.

"I also felt like that," said another girl.

"I wanted to change what I saw," one of the boys said. "I didn't look the way I wanted to. I didn't look like my heroes."

"What is it that you're looking at?" Sensei asked. "When I do this little test with little children, all of them just stare with curiosity at what they see in the mirror. I ask them what they see and they describe their noses or mouth or eyes; just the plain facts of a human face looking out at them. You see that they haven't yet learned to judge them- selves. They see just what's there and when it's gone there's nothing left over in their minds about it. They forget it immediately. They don't carry over the memory of what they saw because they are not disturbed by it. But sometime as they get a little older, and it doesn't take long for it to happen, they start to develop a mental image of themselves. Mostly it is a negative or bad image. And this is because of the way we try to be good. People around us want us to be good so they reward good behavior and punish bad behavior. It's like when you want to train your dog, you scold them when they're bad and you give them a treat when they're good. It's the same with people, but what happens is that trying to be good by making us feel bad about what we do only hurts us.

"So when we look at ourselves in the Mirror of Truth what we often see is someone we don't like. What we also see is another person who we think we should be, the 'good' person people are trying to have us become. This may sound a bit complicated but it makes sense. In other words, the little child has not yet been trained, or conditioned to think of him- or herself as good or bad. They just see what's there, with no mental image to compare it with. But soon they learn to see themselves as someone who is bad, who is not good. This creates conflict inside of themselves, like a 'tug of war' between being bad and good.

"It may take time for you to fully realize this," Sensei went on. "First you need to understand the meaning of what I am saying, like if you had never seen a computer and

I described to you what it was. Then you need to actually confirm what I'm talking about for yourself by trying the computer out. It may take awhile for you to get used to it but, after awhile, with the help of a good teacher, you'll understand how it works. Your brain is like this. Conflict comes from the way you think, which creates the way you feel, which creates how you act. Little kids don't have this conflict between how they should or shouldn't be. It's learned.

"Not only do we form an image of ourselves in this way but we also form images of others too. Remember when we talked about prejudice? Having negative images of ourselves is prejudice. It is a prejudgment, something we've been taught to do. And this conflict in our brains is the conflict out in the world because we are the world and the world is us. We create the world by the way we think and feel. So begin to observe your mind, be aware of your thoughts, watch each one of them to see what they are doing to you and to the world outside you."

That was it. The test was over and the group all passed. But before they could leave, Sensei asked them to sit quietly and to "watch" their thoughts. Henry sat there with the other students and just "looked" at what he was thinking. He saw that most of his thoughts were worries about things in the past or worries about whether such things would happen again in the future. He also became aware of how he wanted to do things that made him happy. As he sat there he wished he were at the pizza restaurant eating a big pizza. He then thought about how eating too much pizza would probably make him sick. Then he remembered the last time he was sick and he began to worry about it happening again and on and on it went, a string of similar thoughts, one triggering another like a row of dominoes falling, knocking the next one and the next. He also became aware of how fast the thoughts triggered feelings and that how he didn't want to feel those feelings and how he began to resist them, which just made it worse. Sitting there watching all these thoughts and feelings he imagined himself sitting in the curl of a great wave, that the wave was made up of all these bits and pieces of thoughts. As long as he just watched the thoughts without trying to change or resist them he felt safe, like a surfer does when riding in the curl of the wave.

He remembered what Mr. Lee had told him once about thinking. He said to try not to think of a white elephant, which just made Henry think of one. The more he tried not

to think of one the more he did. The more he sat watching his thoughts and the feelings that came with them the more he realized that most, if not all, of these thoughts were from the past and were really unnecessary. He realized that worrying did no good. What was past was past and couldn't be changed no matter how hard he tried. He began to understand that certain thoughts were necessary, like thinking about planning his vacation, or about what he had to memorize in his math test at school. But most of what he regretted in the past couldn't be changed and worrying about the future was a waste of time. He felt that the lesson of the Mirror of Truth helped him to look at fear and to see that the only thing to fear was fear itself.

Although he had just passed the test for rank advancement he now knew that the real test was just beginning, the test of life.

Love

Being A Martial Arts Warrior for Peace

10

"Joe Armstrong smashed his first attacker with a crunching kick to the ribs, breaking his bones and sending a few ribs piercing through the skin." Mr. Lee read from a magazine. "He then punched his masked adversary in the eyes, blinding him temporarily so that he staggered back into a wall. Our hero closed in and grabbed the villain by his neck, and with a swift jerk of his powerful arms, snapped it like a twig. Joe then spun around, swooped up the baseball bat that had dropped from his first opponent's hand, and smashed a second attacker. The force of it cracked open the attacker's head, causing his eyes to bulge out. Joe then assailed him with a furious series of punches and kicks that finally caused him to fall backwards with blood running from his mouth.

"All of a sudden a giant of a man came out of the dark alley. Looking like a monster from your worst nightmare, he wielded a sword in each hand and waved them threateningly. Joe stopped, and coolly flexed his muscles, smiling at the creature lurching at him. 'The bigger they come . . .' he smiled to himself. Then, with lightening speed our hero jumped high into the air and kicked the giant right in the throat, at the same time swinging the bat down with both hands to smash the crown of his head. The giant rocked back and forth and rolled his eyes upward; then, like a giant oak tree falling in slow motion, dropped face first to the ground with a tremendous thud. The hero calmly looked at the mangled bad guys littering the ground, satisfied that goodness had once again triumphed over evil. 'They always say that three's a crowd,' he commented."

"Hurrah!" one of the new students began to applaud, but then stopped because of the silence of the others.

"That's OK, you can applaud," said Mr. Lee, smiling. "That's what they want you to do. What I'm reading is a scene from a new action film called *New York Ninja*. The 'hero' beats up the bad guys because the bad guys deserve it. The movie sets you up for this. First there are plenty of scenes where the villains do really terrible things so when the hero does them in, you feel that they got what they deserved. What is wrong with this picture?"

"It seems a little fakey," said one student.

"It seems exaggerated," said Henry.

"Good word!" exclaimed Mr. Lee. "Can you tell us what that means?"

"It means something like beyond the truth," offered Henry.

"Very good, you are both very sharp. It is indeed fake; it is exaggerated; it is 'beyond the truth.' We know people aren't completely evil or completely good. We know people can't survive endless brutal beatings and live. We know people are not invincible. And they don't make jokes when they're in life-threatening situations. It's all written and acted to get you to fear and hate the bad guys and to cheer the hero for killing them. The movie-makers want you to get really worked up; they want you to get excited so you'll pay money to see the next film and the next. Rarely do these action films show you how to resolve conflict peacefully because calm and peaceful movies don't get you all worked up like they want you to be.

"But emotions like fear and anger are very powerful and can get you to say and do things you might not do if you were calm. Think about the news you watch on TV. All kinds of good things and bad things happen in a day, but which do you mostly see on the evening news? Good or bad?"

"Mostly bad," a student called out.

"Right, they show us pretty frightening things every night, because that's what excites us, gets us to watch. But what can happen when we watch these bad things for a long time? We can become used to fear, even addicted to it, which often leads to one of two things: we *need* to watch these bad things because we believe that the world is a fearful place, or we just stop feeling fear altogether. Both of these results are unhealthy.

"So, if you are going to watch these action movies be aware of what they are doing to you. As you watch the movie, 'watch' your emotions. Get in touch with your feelings, see what the movie is making you feel, and then see if those feelings carry over outside the theater. Are you seeing people you don't like as villains like the ones in the movie? Do you have the same emotions of fear and anger about them? It's important to understand what effects you."

"Then are action heroes really bad people?" asked a student.

"Of course not," Mr. Lee laughed. "I mean, they may be good or bad in real life, who knows? But to us they're just actors who make a living by following a script that somebody else wrote. As a matter of fact, I can tell you about one action hero who was really a very wise man, not to mention a great martial artist. Anyone heard of Bruce Lee?"

All of the hands in class shot up.

"He's the greatest," another new student shouted.

"Why is he the greatest? By the way, we are not related," Mr. Lee commented with a smile.

"Because he was so fast. He was really tough," the new student said.

"Do you think that was only in the movies? Wasn't that really make-believe? Do you know what his real contribution was?" Mr. Lee responded.

"He could really kick high and he could take on lots of bad guys," the new student went on. "I think he's really awesome! No one can do what he did."

"Did you ever meet him?" asked another student.

"Yes, I had that pleasure," said Mr. Lee. "And I can tell you that his life and work have been very much misunderstood. Many people consider him violent because he made some action films when he was young. The terrible tragedy is that he died before he could share with the world the real insights he was just beginning to discover. What we are left with are only his films, but also, fortunately, one of his books that tells us what the real martial arts are all about, martial arts that are for peace.

"I am telling you this because you've probably already seen some of his films or will see them and think that he is either some superhuman being or just a violent action-film star. I can tell you that he was neither. He was a very intelligent man and I feel it's important to see the intelligent things he did and not judge him only by his films, for what he was pointing to is of great value, not only in the martial arts but for everyday life.

"Bruce Lee suffered in real life from prejudice because he was Chinese." Mr. Lee went on, talking mainly to the new students. "I think that it's very important not to get caught up in the image the movies have created of him, not to make him some sort of superhero. Many people have made a lot of money using his image in this way. They like the power that comes from being close to someone famous. It's enough for some people even to say that they knew him or even better that they studied with him. But fame is temporary and certainly no guarantee of happiness. It can even be dangerous. So, you may think it's cool to be like Bruce Lee but what you want to be like isn't real. It's what is called a 'myth.' A myth is just a story, not the truth. It's just wishful thinking.

"But Bruce Lee discovered something of great value in the martial arts, something that we are trying to teach you today. He didn't make it up. It was just something he was pointing to, asking us to look at the real value of the martial arts. He was raised in a society that felt that tradition was very important. Tradition means following the old ways without change. Bruce Lee wanted to change things. He was a thinker and a doer. He felt that the physical forms of the martial arts, especially the old Chinese forms, were out of date and were not practical for modern-day self-defense. So he spent a great deal of time and energy studying all sorts of martial arts, including boxing, and came up with an interesting new approach.

"I won't call it a style because that would make it sound like a fixed way of doing things, but rather he came up with a 'perspective,' which means that he realized that in order to be free of any fixed ways he had to be flexible, he had to adapt to what he called 'what is.' This 'what is' meant that a martial artist had to be able to respond to what was happening in that moment and not from any past ideas of what should happen. It's like the cat that when disturbed can move immediately to a new situation without thinking. It just acts. Of course the martial artist, like the cat, has certain 'weapons,' certain abilities in order to defend himself, but when something happens the response is immediate and appropriate to that particular situation."

Without saying a word, Mr. Lee suddenly grabbed the light cushion next to him and threw it at one of the new students. The student ducked and the pillow flew harmlessly over his head.

"There, that's what I mean. If you had thought about what to do, the pillow would have hit you. But instead you did what came naturally and ducked. You 'defeated' the pillow by adapting immediately to a new situation. You obviously knew how to duck, so the 'technique' of ducking was already a part of your defense. But the action to duck was spontaneous, without your having to think, 'Hey, there's a pillow coming at me. What should I do to avoid being hit by it?' It was faster than that. That's what I think Bruce Lee meant.

"He called what he developed Jeet Kune Do, which means the 'Way of the Intercepting Fist.' But then many people tried to learn Jeet Kune Do as a fixed set of techniques and in so doing created a 'style,' a fixed martial arts method that he himself was trying to get away from. Then they made him the 'master' of that style and put him up on a pedestal and worshipped him. But the sad thing about all this is that he was pointing to the need to be flexible, to be free of fixed patterns of self-defense because he was aware of their limitations. He was aware that fixed patterns created a fixed attitude of mind. It was at this point that he discovered the real cause of the problem."

"But why didn't he say that in his movies?" a senior student asked.

"He said it in a book called the *Tao of Jeet Kune Do*. If you read the first twenty pages or so, and understand what's said there, you'll see that he was just beginning to discover something important, something that was beyond physical self-defense. He was beginning to discover the attitude of mind behind the fist, that the way a person thinks can cause conflict inside and around him. Bruce Lee was discovering what is called 'conditioning,' a word we use around here a lot. He started to understand that a person's actions, what a person thinks and therefore does, is controlled by thought.

"For example, if you're in a bad mood it will affect you and the people around you. If you're in conflict, then it will not only hurt you but probably your family and friends too. Bruce Lee began to realize that in order to understand and resolve conflict peacefully you had to understand the way you were taught, or trained, to think. For instance, if you were taught to be afraid of Chinese people, which he felt being Chinese, then

you're in conflict with any Chinese person you meet. You're prejudiced and, as we well know, prejudice has caused terrible suffering in the world. Can you begin to see the value of what he was pointing to?"

"Then why did he make those action films. All I remember that's in them is fighting." the same new student asked.

"That's a good question and I'm not sure I can answer that completely, for I'm not Bruce Lee. But I can give you my opinion. I think that his background, being raised in China had something to do with it. There he experienced a lot of fighting and prejudice. Also, it may have had to do with his father being an actor, so he became an actor when he was young. Perhaps he felt later in life that acting was a way for him to express what he saw in the martial arts. But it is important to remember that he had little control over the production and directing of the movies he was in. He was also young and if he had lived longer perhaps he would have had more control over the movies he made and would have shown us the real martial arts he was beginning to discover.

"Fame and money are powerful temptations. But my feeling is that he would have shown himself to be a true martial artist and not have continued with those types of action films and instead acted in ones that were more intelligent. If I remember correctly, he was thinking about that just before he died.

"But the most important thing is what we do with the realization that conflict is created by the way we think, that we are mostly ignorant of the way we have been conditioned to think. This was what he was beginning to tell us. But this insight doesn't belong to Bruce Lee or anyone. It's just a fact; it's true. Don't accept it because Bruce Lee or anyone tells you it's true. Find out for yourself. Observe your thoughts throughout the day and learn from them. Awareness is your teacher. All anyone can do is to point it out; you have to do the looking. And if it's true, because you have discovered it for yourself, then you will create a better life for yourself and everyone else. And if you're serious you will see beyond his early films and see that this man was a real master of the martial arts, a martial arts champion for peace because his real interest was in helping people understand what creates conflict, and the terrible human suffering it causes.

"At the end of his book," concluded Mr. Lee, "He said, 'Learning Jeet Kune Do is not a matter of seeking knowledge or accumulating a stylized pattern, but in discovering the cause of ignorance.' I'd like you all to think about that."

11 Courage and Commitment

Fighting Injustice

Henry had been attending classes at the martial arts school for the entire school year. Now it was summer and he was being invited to the International Martial Arts for Peace Camp for a special training. Young people had applied to attend from all over the world.

The camp was located deep in the woods by a blue lake. They had traveled for two days to get there. The buildings were nestled into nature as if they had grown there naturally. The days were pleasantly warm with cool nights. The mountain air was light and clean. At night the sky was filled with billions of tiny points of light. It was not possible to think about what that meant because thought just couldn't capture that immensity.

Henry and the other students who had been invited to the camp spent late evenings listening to the crickets. Sitting there the mind was quiet and the spirit renewed.

"Have you ever heard the words 'spiritual' or 'spirit?' Do you know what they mean?" Sensei asked the group one evening as they sat by a fire in the dark, star-filled night.

"Does it mean religious?" a boy from Russia said in perfect English. "I've heard the word before. I think that it has to do with the church."

"Yes, that's one meaning." Sensei answered. "But these words have other meanings. They mean that which belongs to the 'spirit,' which means not physical. It refers to the 'soul' or something that is eternal, that which goes beyond the physical body. I personally think that understanding these two words and the difference between them is very important, even when you're young and you probably think it doesn't matter to you.

"But since you are studying the martial arts that are for peace, these words will have meaning for you now, even if you are not aware of it," Sensei continued.

"I don't want to lecture you. We probably talk too much already, but I just want to touch on this briefly. I am not interested in what most people mean by 'spiritual.' I hear people saying that they want to live a 'spiritual life,' by which they mean a 'good' one. I can understand this. Anyone who is sensitive and intelligent wants goodness in life. But it's the way we try to bring about goodness that is a problem, because we do it through judging our behavior as bad and trying to live up to what we have been told is good. As we discussed before, this only creates more conflict. Let's leave it there.

"But the word 'spirit' is important in the martial arts and life, so I think that we need to say just a little about it. The word 'spirit' in the martial arts means 'courage' and 'commitment.' These two words go together. You will need courage to stand up for what you think is right and commitment to keep on doing it. You will need to be very brave to fight injustice.

"Another word you need to understand is 'honor.' Like most words, it has many meanings. We use the word 'honor' to mean 'to respect' or 'to hold in high regard.' What I am asking you to be aware of is to honor, to respect, the Martial Arts Code of Conduct, not because we are telling you to but because you have seen the importance of it in your lives. You will need to have great courage to do so because there are people who don't want to act properly and resent it if anyone else does.

"Let me quote you a statement that may help you remember this. It comes from Albert Einstein, a man who was not only a great scientist, but perhaps more importantly a great person, who had the courage to stand up for what he thought was right. And he was often criticized about his views. He said: 'Great spirits often encounter violent opposition from mediocre minds.'

"This may sound like arrogance on his part but I think that it's just the truth, a fact, and not his opinion. Here he uses the word 'spirits' to mean people who have stood up for what they feel is right, people with courage who fought injustice.

"Fighting injustice is not always popular. Throughout history people have had to stand up for what was right when it was dangerous for them to do so. During World War

II many young people in Germany stood up against Hitler and the Nazi party. They called themselves the 'White Rose.' During the troubled times of segregation here in America many courageous people stood up against that injustice. There are many, many examples of real heroes, not the fake ones in the movies and on TV, who have been brave and fought injustice.

"If you are really serious and want to be a Black Belt Warrior for Peace, one whose goal is to understand and stop conflict, you will need to first understand how conflict is created. We've tried to teach you something about it at our school and now here at camp. Remember that this is the real purpose of the martial arts that are for peace. If you just want to take the martial arts to win trophies at tournaments or to just learn self-defense to beat up a bully, then you are not a martial artist, you're what I would call a 'martialist,' a person who just wants to learn to fight. But a martial artist that is for peace is a person who takes the intent of all martial arts seriously and wants to understand and stop conflict. I cannot say this often enough.

"You'll need the skills the Martial Arts Code of Conduct can teach you, especially courage and commitment, because without courage and commitment you may know what the problem is, but will not have the energy or drive to find the solution, that is, to do something about it. Now this all may sound 'cool' or romantic but I can tell you to live the Martial Arts Code of Conduct takes great courage and commitment. These skills are skills that a Warrior for Peace needs to do 'battle' for justice, for peace. We do teach you physical self-defense skills to protect yourself, if need be. These are the warrior skills of self-protection. These are defensive skills and are not meant to be used offensively. Hopefully these physical skills will give you the confidence to use your mental self-defense skills first.

"The warrior image frightens many people because to them it means being violent, and this might be true if we were only teaching you physical skills. But as you know, a martial art that is for peace is a whole art, teaching all levels of skills necessary to avoid, resolve, and manage conflict. Many people think that learning physical self-defense skills will only lead to more violence and I say again that's true if that's *all* people are taught.

"Many so-called people of peace think that the martial arts are the opposite of peace. But their approach is to deny the violence in them by judging it as bad and then striving to become good. Peace cannot come through ideals, of wanting to be peaceful. Peace can only come about by understanding what *prevents* it, that is, understanding what creates conflict. And in order to do that you have to see the conflict in action in yourself when it's happening. We need to see the 'martial' in each of ourselves, to have the opportunity to come into direct contact with it without trying to cover it over with judgments of how bad it is. Then and only then is there an opportunity to be free of it. Thinking alone will not do this. In fact only thinking about it can lead to many ways of becoming peaceful, that is, your way versus my way, your belief over my belief. This is what created conflict in the first place and only continues it."

Henry thought that what Sensei said made more sense to him now after all these months of training. When he first joined the school he didn't really understand what his teachers were saying but he had stayed on because he felt that what they were doing was right even if he couldn't put it into words. He now understood why there weren't as many students in his school compared to the one he and his mother visited in the mall. The one in the mall gave the students what they had been conditioned by TV and the movies to want. They played on these Hollywood views to offer what the students thought martial arts training would bring them in life—power and fame. He realized that martial arts that were for peace required a serious commitment and most people were not ready to do this.

Being together at the camp gave Henry and the other students and teachers time to get to know each other better than at the school because they were all together all day long instead of a few hours a week. It gave them time to address real day-to-day issues that came up in relating to each other. It was easier for the students to see what their teachers were saying at the school because they now had the time to live it, to try out what they had learned in a practical, more natural environment.

The camp also gave them time to practice their forms out in nature where they seemed naturally to belong. Doing them in the open area in the woods by the lake gave them a natural sense of their beauty. In this way they could feel the artistic nature of the forms and not focus on them as a means of self-defense. Doing this changed the movements from fighting forms to art forms, from a way to protect themselves to an expression of inner power and grace.

The summer went by with a swiftness that made each day seem precious. Much time was spent in just talking to each other and the teachers, for some martial arts teachers also came with their students from other parts of the world. Henry was amazed at how similar they all were no matter what country they came from. He realized that intelligent people were everywhere and that because they were intelligent that the usual artificial barriers no longer separated them into "we" and "them."

It was a time of hard work and leisure. The leisure was not just resting or not working. It was a time to enjoy life, to be quiet enough to let life teach them. It was not a wasted time, as some people might think, but a time of great productivity. It was not the productivity of gaining something but rather of letting go of all the self-imposed demands that people put on themselves. It was a time of real learning, not the learning of accumulating facts and information but the learning that comes from moment-to-moment awareness of their states of mind. It was this moment-to-moment awareness that allowed them to observe the root of conflict in the way they all had been conditioned to think. It was this leisure that brought about a real change in their behavior, not out of force, but out of intelligence.

They now were beginning to have a means by which they could understand what was meant by the "Art of Empty Self." This leisure allowed for an "emptying" of their pre-judgments that caused conflict in their lives and in the world. They were beginning to realize that what they called their "selves" was only a collection of memories, some of which were practical and necessary to live, and others that were unnecessary and destructive. They could, through observing their own thought processes, see that the cause of conflict was who they thought they were, their conditioned prejudices, ingrained by the many influences on their lives. If they were going to be able to lead a healthy and peaceful life it was dawning on Henry and the other students that understanding the martial arts that were for peace was of great importance. Their teachers could only point this out; the rest was completely up to them. They realized that conflict was a part of life and what they did with it was what mattered.

The last night at camp Sensei called all the students and teachers together into the main room and read them a few stories from his books. At the end of this he sat quietly with them for a few minutes.

"I am happy all of you could come to the camp again this year," he finally said. "It's wonderful to see people from all over the world who are interested in martial arts that are for peace. I hope that we have increased your understanding of the potential these fine arts of peace have to offer, not just through understanding the words we use, although that's the first step in understanding anything, but by being able to see the truth of it in your own lives. I hope you have been able, or will be able, to work through all these stages of learning, from understanding the explanation, to reflecting on the personal examples in your life, to the experience of immediate awareness of what is happening in the moment. In this way you're not just memorizing what we've said, and are either rejecting it or modifying it because it doesn't fit with your view of what peace means. But rather you understand what prevents peace, and what creates conflict, not because we have convinced you of it, but because you have actually seen its real value in your day-to-day lives.

"If this is so then we have done our jobs well in educating you to meet the challenges of life with a brave warrior's spirit, as a Black Belt Warrior for Peace. I leave you with one final question, for it's the question not answered that will lead to awareness and to freedom. Remember to ask yourself, when facing any of life's many challenges, 'What is the intelligent thing to do?'"

12 Respect

Honoring the Dignity of All Life

Henry grew up that year. He continued taking classes at his martial arts school for many years and finally received his first-degree black belt. He went on to second and third degree and today is an assistant martial arts teacher at his school, helping Ms. Watts, Mr. Lee, and Sensei, who was getting older.

Henry learned many things studying peaceful martial arts, but the most important of these was respect: honoring the dignity of all life, treating all things with care and sensitivity. He realized that in the natural world everyone and everything has its place and purpose. The lone, tiny ant crawling along the floor is as special as the distant stars in the universe; everything in the natural world is somehow connected in a mysterious web of relationships, and if you disturb one thread of that web it affects the whole.

He also understood that humans can become confused and do harmful things to each other and to the earth and the livings things that inhabit it. He realized that people create an unnatural world and suffer for it because of their ignorance; they hurt themselves and others because they are not aware of what they are doing and the effect their actions have on life around them. He understood that people are born innocent but become conditioned to think mainly of themselves and their own survival because they are afraid.

He understood how fear creates darkness and intelligence brings the light of understanding and acceptance. He realized that people who are conditioned are confused and ignorant, and are not to be blamed. He discovered that to live a meaningful life is to help educate, to bring an understanding of how this ignorance and confusion creates so much conflict and suffering in the world. He also realized that martial arts that are for peace can, if taught correctly, be a way for people to learn about themselves and to live a more intelligent, loving life.

Although he had practiced diligently the physical skills of the martial arts, what impressed Henry the most was how Sensei related those to the mental martial arts, how he taught the martial arts as a whole art, combining the mental and physical to create a martial art that was for peace and self-understanding. He wished that everyone could experience that because he knew that the world would be a better place because of it. He remembered most of all a story Sensei had read to the class at the summer camp the first year Henry started taking martial arts. The story had helped him to understand his place in life and showed him a path to a life of dignity and respect. Sensei had called the story "The Flight of the Golden Eagle."

Henry remembered Sensei beginning, "Have you ever watched a bird soar on the air, wings spread out, floating upward, so easily, effortlessly, gliding free in the beauty of endless sky? Remember wishing you were free also, soaring up above the earth with no cares, no worries? Sometimes people are so earthbound, so full of worries, the stress and strain of daily life, it's like they have blinders on, like horses trained to look only straight ahead, and place one foot after another.

"People are often so afraid. Few ever break free to soar like an eagle, high above the rest. Held back by their own self-created prisons, people think that life itself, their own situation, or another person is holding them back. They don't realize that their prison is their own mind, that they are trapped only because they think they are. People have been conditioned to think in ways that limit their lives. But there are some who fly, who break out of the imaginary cages that hold them, because they realize that there are no cages!

"Imagine a little bird that is captured and put into a cage when it is young," Sensei had continued. "It only knows the world inside its little prison and has forgotten the greater world outside. One day someone leaves the cage door open. The bird senses this